SCIENCE
NEWS
for
KIDS

Health and Medicine

SCIENCE NEWS for KIDS

Computers and Technology

Earth Science

The Environment

Food and Nutrition

Health and Medicine

Space and Astronomy

SCIENCE NEWS for KIDS

Health and Medicine

Series Editor
Tara Koellhoffer

With a Foreword by
Emily Sohn,
Science News for Kids

CHELSEA CLUBHOUSE
An Imprint of Chelsea House Publishers

Health and Medicine

Chelsea Clubhouse
An imprint of Chelsea House Publishers
132 West 31st Street
New York NY 10001

For Library of Congress Cataloging-in-Publication Data, please contact the publisher.

ISBN 0-7910-9122-8

Chelsea House books are available at special discounts when purchased in bulk quantities for businesses, associations, institutions, or sales promotions. Please call our Special Sales Department in New York at (212) 967-8800 or (800) 322-8755.

You can find Chelsea House on the World Wide Web at
http://www.chelseahouse.com

Text and cover design by Takeshi Takahashi
Layout by Ladybug Editorial & Design

Printed in the United States of America

Bang   10 9 8 7 6 5 4 3 2 1

This book is printed on acid-free paper.

All links, web addresses, and Internet search terms were checked and verified to be correct at the time of publication. Because of the dynamic nature of the web, some addresses and links may have changed since publication and may no longer be valid.

Contents Overview

Detailed Table of Contents

Detailed Table of Contents

by Emily Sohn
Science News for Kids

Science, for many kids, is just another subject in school. You may have biology tests and astronomy quizzes to study for, chemistry formulas to memorize, physics problems to work through, or current events to report on. All of it, after a while, can seem like a major drag.

Now, forget about all that, and think about your day. What did you eat for breakfast? How did you get to school and what did you think about along the way? What makes the room bright enough for you to see this book? How does the room stay cool or warm enough for you to be comfortable? What do you like to do for fun?

All of your answers, in some way, involve science. Food, transportation, electricity, toys, video games, animals, plants, your brain, the rest of your body: Behind the scenes of nearly anything you can think of, there are scientists trying to figure out how it works, how it came to be, or how to make it better. Science can explain why pizza and chocolate taste good. Science gives airplanes a lift. And science is behind the medicines that make your aches and pains go away. Most exciting of all, science never stands still.

Science News for Kids tracks the trends and delves into the discoveries that make life more interesting and more efficient every day. The stories in these volumes explore a tiny fraction of the grand scope of research happening around the world. These stories point out the questions that push scientists to probe ever deeper into physics, chemistry, biology, psychology, and more. Reading about the challenges of science will spark in you the same sort of curiosity that drives researchers to keep searching for answers, despite setbacks and failed experiments. The stories here may even inspire you to seek out your own solutions to the world's puzzles.

Being a scientist is hard work, but it can be one of the best jobs around. You may picture scientists always tinkering away in their labs, pouring chemicals into flasks and reading technical papers. Well, they do those things some of the time. But they also get to dig around in the dirt, blow things up, and even ride rockets into outer space. They travel around the world. They save lives. And, they get to spend most of their time thinking about the things that fascinate them most, all in the name of work.

Sometimes, researchers have revelations that change the way we think about the universe. Albert Einstein, for one, explained light, space, time, and other aspects of the physical world in radically new terms. He's perhaps the most famous scientist in history, thanks to his theories of relativity and other ideas. Likewise, James Watson and

Francis Crick forever changed the face of medicine when they first described the structure of the genetic material DNA in 1953. Today, doctors use information about DNA to explain why some people are likely to develop certain diseases and why others may have trouble reading or doing math. Police investigators rely on DNA to solve mysteries when they analyze hairs, blood, saliva, and remains at the scene of a crime. And scientists are now eagerly pursuing potential uses of DNA to cure cancer and other diseases.

Science can be about persistence and courage as much as it is about grand ideas. Society doesn't always welcome new ideas. Before Galileo Galilei became one of the first people to point a telescope at the sky in the early 1600s, for example, nearly everyone believed that the planets revolved around Earth. Galileo discovered four moons orbiting Jupiter. He saw that Venus has phases, like the moon. And he noticed spots on the sun and lumps on the moon's craggy face. All of these observations shook up the widely held view that the heavens were perfect, orderly, and centered on Earth. Galileo's ideas were so controversial, in fact, that he was forced to deny them to save his life. Even then, he was sentenced to imprisonment in his own home.

Since Galileo's time, the public has so completely accepted his views of the universe that space missions have been named after him, as have craters on the moon and on Mars. In 1969, Neil Armstrong became the first person to stand on the moon. Now, astronauts spend months in orbit, living on an international space station, floating in weightlessness. Spacecraft have landed on planets and moons as far away as Saturn. One probe recently slammed into a comet to collect information. With powerful telescopes, astronomers continue to spot undiscovered moons in our solar system, planets orbiting stars in other parts of our galaxy, and evidence of the strange behavior of black holes. New technologies continue to push the limits of what we can detect in outer space and what we know about how the universe formed.

Here on Earth, computer technology has transformed society in a short period of time. The first electronic digital computers, which appeared in the 1940s, took up entire rooms and weighed thousands of pounds. Decades passed before people started using their own PCs (personal computers) at home. Laptops came even later.

These days, it's hard to imagine life without computers. They track restaurant orders. They help stores process credit cards. They allow you to play video games, send e-mails and instant messages to your friends, and write reports that you can edit and print without ever picking up a pen. Doctors use computers to diagnose their patients, and banks use computers to keep track of our money. As computers become more and more popular, they continue to get smaller, more power-ful, less expensive, and more integrated into our lives in ways we don't even notice.

Probes that fly to Pluto and computers the size of peas are major advances that don't happen overnight. Science is a process of small steps, and a new discovery often starts with a single question. Why, for example, do hurricanes and tsunamis form? What is it like at the cen-ter of Earth? Why do some types of french fries taste bet-ter than others? Research projects can also begin with observations. There are fewer tigers in India than there used to be, for instance. Kids now weigh more than they did a generation ago. Mars shows signs that the planet once supported life.

The next step is investigation, which can take on many forms, depending on the subject. Brain researchers, for one, often do experiments in their labo-ratories with the help of sophisticated equipment. In one type of neuroscience study, subjects repeatedly solve tasks while machines measure activity in their brains. Some environmental scientists who study climate, on the other hand, collect data by tracking weather patterns over the years. Paleontologists dig deep into the earth to look for clues about what the world was like when dinosaurs were alive. Anthropologists learn about other cultures by talking to people and collecting stories. Doctors monitor large numbers of patients taking a new drug or no drug to figure out whether a drug is safe and effective before others can use it.

Designing studies requires creativity, and scientists spend many years training to use the tools of their profession. Physicists need to learn complicated mathematical formulas. Ecologists make models that simulate interactions between species. Physicians learn the name of every bone and blood vessel in the body. The most basic tools, however, are ones that everyone has: our senses. The best way to start learning about the world through science is to pay attention to what you smell, taste, see, hear, and feel. Notice. Ask questions. Collect data. Do experiments. Draw tentative conclusions. Ask more questions.

Most importantly, leave no stone unturned. There's no limit to the topics available for research. Robots, computers, and new technologies in medicine are the waves of the future. Just as important, however, are studies of the past. Figuring out what Earth's climate used to be like and which animals and plants used to live here are the first steps toward understanding how the planet is changing and what those changes might mean for our future. And don't forget to look around at what's going on around you, right now. You might just be surprised at how many subjects you can find to investigate.

Ready to get started? The stories in this book are great sources of inspiration. Each of the articles comes directly from the *Science News for Kids* Website, which you can find online at *http://sciencenewsforkids.org*. All articles at the site, which is updated weekly, cover current events in science, and all are written with middle-school students in mind. If anything you read in this book sparks your interest, feel free to visit the Website to check out the latest developments and find out more.

And keep an eye out for an occasional feature called "News Detective." These essays describe what it's like to be a science journalist, roaming the world in search of scientists at work. Science writing is an often-overlooked career possibility, but science writers have endless opportunities to learn about many things at once, to share in the excitement of scientific discovery, and to help scientists get the word out about the significance of their work.

So, go ahead and turn the page. There's so much left to discover.

Section 1

Diseases and Disorders

The science of health and medicine is vitally important not only for protecting us against deadly diseases, but also for easing the aches and pains of less severe, but still unpleasant, conditions. Medical scientists devote their careers to finding cures for devastating illnesses and to researching for ways to make our daily lives better. In this section, we explore some of the latest developments in health science, from the struggle to stop worldwide epidemic disease to efforts to help people who snore.

The first article explores the danger of a massive, worldwide epidemic, and the steps health scientists are taking to try to prevent it from happening. The second article examines a disease that has already threatened people and animals on a global scale–bovine spongiform encephalopathy, better known as mad cow disease.

The third article explains that the way the brain sends its signals may help doctors determine whether a person is suffering from an attention disorder, while the fourth article describes the serious effects snoring—a seemingly inconsequential problem—can have on your health.

In the fifth article, author Emily Sohn uncovers new research that exposes a possible genetic cause for the reading disorder dyslexia, and, in the final article, we explore the dangers of allergies and new ways to treat and prevent them.

—The Editor

Opposite: This is a photograph taken of the virus that causes SARS, a disease that became an epidemic in early 2003, at a magnification of 300,000X.

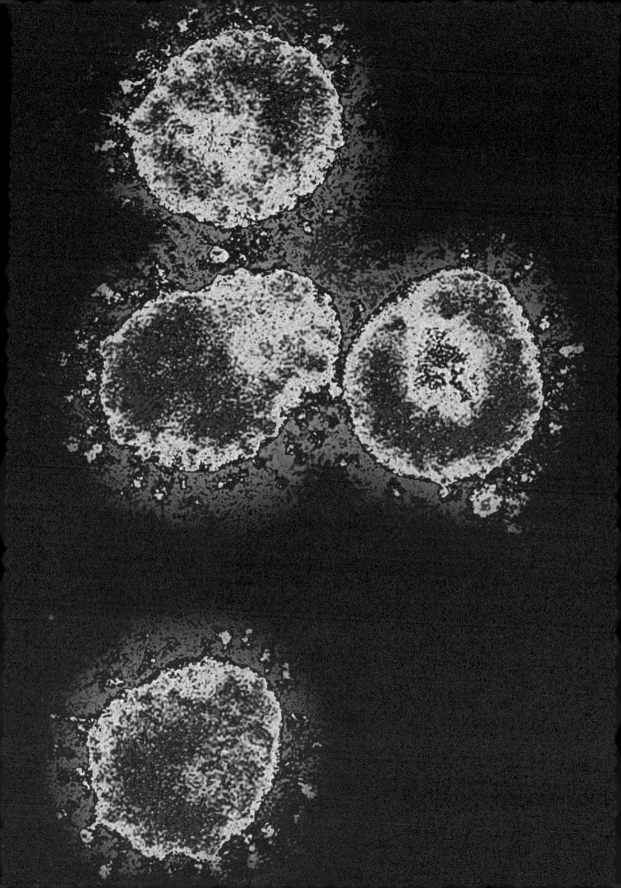

Stopping Deadly Diseases

Diseases tend to make big news, especially when they claim lives and send waves of fear throughout the world, as the SARS (severe acute respiratory syndrome) outbreak did in 2003. Whenever a new illness breaks out, medical professionals called epidemiologists get to work to identify the source of the disease and to find ways to stop it before it can do further damage. In this article, writer Emily Sohn takes a look at the science of epidemiology, highlighting the courageous efforts of the scientists who wage war against disease.

–The Editor

Fighting Off Micro-Invader Epidemics

by Emily Sohn

Before Reading:

- **How do you catch the flu? Where does it come from?**

- **Why do we usually get chickenpox only once in a lifetime?**

Every year when school starts, you hear it in the classroom: a cough here, a snuffle there. Some weeks, more than half your class may be sneezing or hacking away. Colds spread quickly, passing from person to person. Then there's the flu season: sore throats, runny noses, fevers, aches and pains, and absences from school.

It could be worse. In early 2003, many people died in China and other countries from a disease called SARS (severe acute respiratory syndrome). Some schools and hospitals in Toronto, Canada, and elsewhere had to shut down for days to help keep the disease from spreading.

And if you've been following the news lately, you may have heard about the dangers of not only SARS but also monkeypox, mad cow disease, and the West Nile virus. Animals have died. People have gotten sick. Sometimes, panic has set in.

The culprits responsible for most of these ailments are tiny, tiny organisms called **viruses**. Unlike people, animals, and plants, viruses are not made up of cells, but they do contain some of the building blocks of cells. The most important pieces are the molecules **DNA** and **RNA**: sets of instructions that tell cells how to make more cells of the same kind. A virus carries instructions for making more viruses.

- What are some of the main building blocks of cells? Which ones are important for viruses?

When certain viruses invade your body's cells, they can cause your body to react, and you get sick. Your body gets so busy making new copies of a virus that it can't do what it's supposed to do. And when viruses spread easily from person to person or from animal to person, a disease **epidemic** may occur.

- What is the difference between a virus and an epidemic?

RESPECT FOR MICROBES

In the midst of the SARS outbreak in the spring of 2003, I came down with a horrible cold that kept getting worse. Many of my symptoms sounded like SARS. My lungs hurt. I had a sharp cough. I felt feverish. Terrified, I rushed to the doctor. When he told me I had bronchitis,

I was relieved. I still felt miserable, but my fear of having SARS had far outweighed any suffering I felt from bronchitis.

But we don't have to be scared all the time. By arming ourselves with knowledge and adopting a few good habits, experts say, people can stay healthy and strong. We might even learn a few things about the invisible world around us.

The first lesson is respect, says Amy Vollmer, a **microbiologist** at Swarthmore College in Swarthmore, Pennsylvania.

"We survive on this planet not because we're superior," Vollmer says. **Bacteria** and viruses far outnumber us, and the tiny organisms have been here a lot longer than we have.

"**Microbes** have been on the planet for 4 billion years. Humans have been here for a million or so," Vollmer says. "They were here first. We have developed and survived around them."

Most microbes don't affect us at all. Some actually help keep us healthy. But the ones that get our attention are the ones that make us sick, especially if they can easily jump from one person to another.

Our **immune systems** help protect us against such microscopic invaders. These systems are like soccer players: They get better with practice.

When an infectious **pathogen** attacks your body for the first time, you might get really sick for about a week, while your immune system gears up to fight back. The next time you face the same virus, though, your body remembers what to do. Your immune system takes only a few days to kick into gear. You might not even feel any symptoms.

• **How are we able to fight off viruses when they attack?**

Vaccines such as flu shots take advantage of this gearing up. They expose your body to a little bit of a disease, which gives your immune system a dress rehearsal for fighting the invader in case of a more serious attack later on.

IDENTIFYING THE CULPRIT

In recent years, infectious diseases such as SARS and monkeypox have become more common all over the world, says parasitologist Peter Daszak of the Consortium for Conservation Medicine in Palisades, New York. The trend is probably our own fault, he says.

• **Why do we have vaccines?**

"Diseases evolved to be very good at moving from one population to another," Daszak says. "It's what they do best. What we're doing now is creating ways for them to move like they've never done before."

Many people get sick when they take trips to exotic

places where they encounter unfamiliar microbes. If it takes a few days before infected travelers show symptoms, they can spread a disease without knowing it. Some people may even carry and spread a virus without ever getting sick themselves.

When a new epidemic first shows up, scientists start looking for its source. They conduct interviews to uncover patterns about where patients have been or what they've eaten. At the same time, doctors keep infected people in isolation to try to stop the disease from spreading. During the SARS outbreak, people in Asia wore surgical masks in public so they wouldn't inhale the virus.

Next, scientists race to identify the culprit by extracting it from an infected person and testing whether it can cause an infection. When researchers are sure of the cause, biochemical analysis begins.

Investigations quickly showed SARS to be caused by a **coronavirus**, one of many different families of viruses. Analyses of the monkeypox virus revealed that monkeypox is related to a horrible disease called smallpox. This kind of information can help scientists narrow their search for the right kind of drugs or vaccines to prevent future outbreaks.

ANIMAL LINKS

As scientists learn more about disease epidemics, animals turn out to be a vital link.

SARS, for example, started out as a disease in palm civets. A palm civet is a badger-like mammal with spotted fur and a long tail that lives in southern Asia and tropical Africa. Now, researchers have found that cats and ferrets can carry the SARS virus, but no one is sure whether they can spread it to people.

Mosquitoes transmit the West Nile virus. Monkeypox first spread to people in the midwestern United States through pet prairie dogs. The disease had previously appeared only in western Africa.

Yet, animals might be as much a casualty as a cause of epidemics, Daszak says. Diseases may be spreading more often from animals to people simply because people are handling animals without being careful enough, he says.

"We shouldn't really blame animals," Daszak says. "We should blame humans that change animal habitats, humans that trade animals and move them from one place to another, and humans that destroy forests and invade animal homes."

By protecting animals, he says, we also protect ourselves.

For now, all the talk about disease epidemics doesn't mean you need to hide inside all day long. "The best way to stay healthy with all these diseases is to know about them," Daszak says. "It's really fascinating rather than scary."

Simple precautions can make a big difference. Avoid mosquitoes to protect yourself from the West Nile virus. To prevent monkeypox, don't buy exotic animals. If you do want an exotic pet, have a doctor screen it for diseases first.

It also really helps if you wash your hands a lot. And, if you're sick, you should stay away from school and other people.

Most important of all, Vollmer says, is to take care of yourself. By eating well and sleeping enough, your immune system will stay nice and strong.

"If you can learn that early and keep it up as you get older," she says, "you can live a long and healthy life."

- **Where did monkeypox first emerge?**

- **What are some precautions we can take to protect ourselves from viruses?**

- **How do you keep your immune system working smoothly?**

After Reading:

- Microbiologist Amy Vollmer claims that we haven't survived on the planet out of sheer strength or superiority. Why do you think she believes this? What evidence does she use to support her idea?

- Why do scientists, after a new epidemic emerges, immediately try to locate its source?

- How might protecting animals help us reduce the chances of getting infected by viruses?

The Danger of Mad Cow Disease

You've probably heard about the terrifying outbreaks of what's been called "mad cow disease"—a deadly illness that eats away at the brains of affected animals and infects the beef that human beings consume. But what exactly *is* mad cow disease, and what dangers does it pose to people? In the next article, Sorcha McDonagh examines this emerging illness and the steps scientists are taking to try to stop it.

—The Editor

Protecting Cows–and People–
From a Deadly Disease

by Sorcha McDonagh

Chomping at a juicy hamburger might be a little less tempting than it once seemed. It took just one case of mad cow disease, discovered in December 2003, to make several countries ban imports of U.S. beef. Officials in Japan and elsewhere are afraid that people may eat infected meat and develop the human version of mad cow disease.

Mad cow disease gets its name because cattle infected with it behave strangely. They seem nervous and distressed. They can't stand or walk properly.

These symptoms are caused by the breakdown of the animal's nervous system. Deformed proteins, known as **prions**, multiply and worm their way through an infected cow's brain and nerves, making the tissue look like a sponge.

These prions have a similar effect in people. They can cause the fatal human disease known as variant Creutzfeldt-Jakob disease (vCJD). Eating infected beef is the only known way for the prions to go from a cow to a person.

Consuming infected meat is also the main way prions

are transferred from one cow to another. This can happen because of an old method of producing food for cows. When cows were slaughtered for their meat and hides, some of their remains–including their brains, eyes, spinal cords, and intestines–used to be processed to make animal feed containing protein.

This type of feed was banned in 1997 when scientists realized that it was responsible for the spread of mad cow disease.

Christl Donnelly of Imperial College in London says that as long as the ban on this type of feed is enforced, mad cow disease shouldn't spread in the United States. This means it's also highly unlikely the disease would spread to people.

Officials at the U.S. Department of Agriculture are taking an extra precaution. They're planning on tracking every cow that will be used for beef, from its birth until it ends up in the grocery store.

Going Deeper:

Harder, Ben. "Cow Madness: Disease's U.S. Emergence Highlights Role of Feed Ban." *Science News* 165(January 10, 2004): 19–20. Available online at *http://www.sciencenews.org/ 20040110/fob2.asp*.

Milius, Susan. "Mad Cow Future: Tests Explore Next Generation of Defenses." *Science News* 163 (May 31, 2003): 340. Available online at *http:// www.sciencenews.org/20030531/fob3.asp*.

Raloff, Janet. "Calling All Cows." *Science News Online* (October 4, 2003). Available online at *http://www.sciencenews.org/20031004/food.asp*.

You can learn more about mad cow disease online at *http://kidshealth.org/kid/talk/qa/ mad_cow_disease.html* and *http:// faculty.washington.edu/chudler/bse.html*.

Diagnosing Attention-Deficit/Hyperactivity Disorder

It seems like attention-deficit/hyperactivity disorder (ADHD) is always in the news these days. For the people who suffer from ADHD—most of them children and young adults—it is very real, but for years, scientists have not been able to figure out exactly what causes this condition. In the next article, Emily Sohn explores a recent study that discovered some interesting new facts about the brains of people who have ADHD, which may lead to great breakthroughs in treating this devastating disorder.

—The Editor

Brain Signals Attention Disorder

by Emily Sohn

Do you have trouble paying attention in school? Would you rather do 137 things at once than focus on one task a time? Does your body scream to jump up and run around every time you're asked to sit still? If so, the problem might be reflected in your brain.

You probably know at least a few kids who have trouble with concentration, self-control, and organization. (You might even be one of these kids yourself.) In fact, 3 to 6% of schoolchildren in the United States have **attention-deficit/hyperactivity disorder** (**ADHD**). Scientists want to know what goes on in the brains of people with ADHD so that they might find better ways to treat it.

In one recent study, researchers from the University of California, Los Angeles School of Medicine scanned the brains of 73 young people, ages 8 to 18. Twenty-seven of them had ADHD. Forty-six did not.

Children and teenagers with ADHD had less tissue in certain parts of their brain, called the **prefrontal** and **temporal lobes**, the study found. These kids also had extra tissue called **gray matter** in the cortex, or outer layer, in the back of the brain.

The results so far are somewhat puzzling. No one yet has a clear idea of what size differences in certain brain features might have to do with attention disorders. Scientists need more clues to try to figure out why some kids can sit still in the library while others have to be out on the playground.

Going Deeper:

Bower, Bruce. "ADHD's Brain Trail: Cerebral Clues Emerge for Attention Disorder." *Science News* 164 (November 29, 2003): 339. Available online at *http://www.sciencenews.org/20031129/ fob1.asp*.

Information for kids about attention disorders can be found at the Attention Deficit Disorder Association's "Kid's Area" online at *http://www.add.org/content/kids1.htm*.

Does Snoring Affect Your Grades?

For many years, scientists have understood that when people snore, they are not always getting the highest-quality sleep possible. A lot of research has been devoted to finding out why people snore and looking for ways to prevent snoring to help people sleep better. One study, however, looked at another aspect of snoring—how it affects the brain and the way snorers function in everyday life. According to the following article, some scientists believe snoring may not only cause problems sleeping, but may lead to changes in the brain itself, which can bring about problems with learning and might even be a factor in the development of ADHD.

—The Editor

Grades Slipping? Check for Snoring

by Emily Sohn

Disappointed with your performance on the last spelling test? Stop snoring!

Kids who always snore when they sleep are four times more likely to get bad grades in school than are students who never snore, according to a new study.

A group of German scientists asked the parents of 1,129 third-graders whether their children snored always, frequently, occasionally, or never. The researchers also collected information about how well the students did in school.

Frequent and constant snorers did worse in math, science, and spelling than did occasional snorers and non-snorers, the data showed.

The researchers also tested whether the snorers might have a sleep disorder called **intermittent hypoxia**. Caused by low levels of oxygen in the blood, this disorder is fairly common. People who have it often snore. Still, kids who had the disorder didn't get worse grades than did kids without it, the second study showed.

Snoring might just keep kids from sleeping well, the researchers think. Being tired would make it hard to pay attention and perform well in school. So, make sure to tell your doctor if you snore a lot. If the problem is extreme, surgery to remove the **tonsils** sometimes helps.

Whatever you do, don't start snoring while you're at school. Then, you'll really be in trouble!

Going Deeper:

Seppa, Nathan. "Grades Slipping? Check for Snoring." *Science News* 164 (September 13, 2003): 173–174. Available online at *http://www.sciencenews.org/20030913/note13.asp*.

You can learn more about snoring online at *http://kidshealth.org/kid/health_problems/teeth/snoring.html*.

Is Dyslexia in the DNA?

As scientists learn more and more about the genes and how different traits are passed from one generation to the next, they are also finding out that specific diseases and disorders may be transmitted in the genes, just like hair or eye color. As the next article demonstrates, a recent study examined the possibility that the reading disorder dyslexia may be caused by a mutation on a specific human gene.

—The Editor

A DNA Clue to Reading Troubles

by Emily Sohn

If you tend to feel like you just weren't born to read, you might be right.

Scientists have identified the first gene involved in some cases of **dyslexia**, a learning disorder that affects at least 1 in 25 people. People with dyslexia have trouble with spelling, reading, writing, explaining their thoughts in words, and understanding sounds within words.

Cells in your body contain long molecules called DNA, which provide instructions for making materials called proteins. Roughly speaking, a stretch of DNA that makes a specific protein is known as a **gene**. If a gene is defective, it could produce the wrong protein and cause something in your body not to work properly.

In their search for genes involved in dyslexia, scientists had previously narrowed their focus to a few stretches of DNA that held tens or hundreds of genes. Within one of those regions, a group of Swedish researchers found a gene mutation in certain members of a Finnish family. The father, who was dyslexic, and his two dyslexic daughters all had a **mutation** in a gene called DYXC1.

Then, the researchers broadened their study to look at 109 children and adults diagnosed with dyslexia and 195 people without the learning disorder. Results showed that 9% of those with dyslexia had the DYXC1 mutation, compared with fewer than 3% of the other group. A different kind of DYXC1 mutation appeared in 12% of the dyslexic group, compared with only 5% of the others. Scientists now have to figure out how the gene and its protein work.

DYXC1 is clearly not the only gene involved in dyslexia, the researchers say. Still, they hope their findings will help doctors diagnose and treat people with the learning disorder.

Going Deeper:

Bower, Bruce. "Dyslexia's DNA Clue: Gene Takes Stage in Learning Disorder." *Science News* 164 (August 30, 2003): 131. Available online at *http://www.sciencenews.org/20030830/fob1.asp*.

You can learn more about dyslexia online at *http://kidshealth.org/kid/health_problems/ learning_problem/dyslexia.html* and *http:// faculty.washington.edu/chudler/dyslexia.html*.

All About Allergies

Like most people, you may have an allergy to something, such as tree pollen, dust, or pet dander. In general, allergies are just a nuisance that people have to deal with, usually at certain times of the year, such as the spring when pollen is abundant in the air. For some people, however, allergies are much more serious. In fact, they can be life- threatening. This article explores some of the most common allergens (substances that cause allergic reactions) and what can be done to prevent them or at least ease the symptoms.

—The Editor

Allergies: From Bee Stings to Peanuts

by Emily Sohn

Before Reading:

- **Name eight foods or other substances that can cause allergies.**

- **What signs tell you that someone may be suffering an allergic reaction to pollen, a bee sting, or a certain food?**

The bee sting hurt so much that I stopped my bike just to yelp. I checked the swelling on my thigh to make sure the stinger was gone. Then I kept on biking.

About 15 minutes later, my ears and armpits started to itch like crazy. A rash appeared on my arms. My lips and eyelids began to puff up. Pretty soon, I had to get off my bike because I was having trouble breathing. My chest felt constricted. My heart was racing. Itchy welts were popping up all over my body and inside my throat. My eyes were starting to swell shut.

In a panic, I grabbed my cell phone and called 911. I was having a severe allergic reaction to the bee sting. Without help, I knew there was a chance I could die.

"More people die from bee stings than from dog bites

every year," a doctor told me when I finally arrived in the emergency room after a nerve-wracking ambulance ride.

"**Allergies** in general are increasing in the population," says Marc McMorris. He's a pediatric allergist at the University of Michigan Health System in Ann Arbor.

More than 50 million people in the United States have serious allergies (Figure 1.1). And not just to bees. Food allergies cause even more deaths than bee stings, McMorris says.

Figure 1.1 Millions of people have allergies, many of them to certain common allergens, such as nuts, bees, and flowers.

Allergies to peanuts, in particular, are on the rise, along with reactions to ragweed, mosses, molds, cats, dogs, and shellfish. Name just about anything, and you'll probably find someone allergic to it.

PUZZLING DETAILS

As more and more people develop allergies, researchers are trying to understand what causes allergic reactions. Their hope is to find better ways of treating and preventing such reactions, which can sometimes be life-threatening.

- **How many people in the United States have allergies that are considered serious?**

Many details remain mysterious, however. It's not clear, for example, why different people react to different things, even within the same family.

"I treat a family with eight children, and they're all allergic to some degree," McMorris says. "Some have asthma, some have **eczema**, some have bee allergies. They're all different. It's just by chance that one person is allergic to one thing, while another person is allergic to something else."

An allergy begins when the body encounters a foreign object, such as **pollen**, nut proteins, or bee venom. At first exposure, the body's immune system reacts as if the object were a germ or parasite. It produces proteins called **antibodies**, which fight the intruder, or **allergen**.

After your body makes the type of antibodies that trigger allergies, these antibodies stick around in your bloodstream as a sort of memory of the incident. After that, if you're prone to allergies, repeated exposure to the same allergen can cause your immune system to freak out.

> • **Describe how your body creates an allergy.**

That's exactly what happened to me. I had been stung by plenty of bees in the past. On those occasions, the area around the attack swelled up like a marshmallow in a microwave. This time, though, as soon as the bee venom entered my bloodstream, antibodies latched onto cells in my blood. These cells then released chemicals called **histamines**, which caused the swelling, itching, wheezing, and other symptoms. Severe reactions like mine are called **anaphylaxis**.

Now that the antibodies in my blood are primed to react to bee venom, every sting I get in the future will probably cause an even worse reaction.

In some ways, though, I feel lucky. At least, I'm not allergic to peanuts.

TROUBLING PEANUTS

People with supersensitive peanut allergies can have anaphylactic reactions just from being in the same room as peanut dust. My friend Karen, for one, can't eat jelly if you used the peanut-butter knife to spread it.

"I've had kids react after being licked by someone's dog who just ate dog food with peanut butter in it," McMorris says.

More than 1.5 million Americans are allergic to peanuts. This number is growing, but nobody knows why. One possible cause is that pregnant women and nursing mothers may be eating peanuts before their babies have strong enough immune systems to cope with peanut proteins.

Peanut butter might be another big problem, suggests one recent study by the U.S. Department of Agriculture. The United States lags behind China and India in peanut butter production. But people in the United States have more peanut allergies. That might be because U.S. producers dry roast peanuts instead of boiling them, the new study suggests. Dry roasting appears to change the peanut protein into a form that triggers a more powerful allergic reaction.

Some scientists have been working to develop new strains of peanuts that are less likely to provoke an allergic attack. Other researchers are searching for new vaccines to prevent allergies from developing in the first place. One drug that shows promise was identified in 2003.

- **What are two possible causes of the increase in peanut allergies?**

BEING CAREFUL

For now, awareness and preparation are the best weapons, McMorris says. Some schools are banning peanut butter and jelly sandwiches in their lunchrooms. Allergic people are encouraged to carry special shot dispensers called **epipens**® with them at all times.

I now have two epipens that I'll jab into my leg next time I get stung. I also carry Benadryl®, which blocks the action of histamines. The paramedics that rescued me after the bee sting put in a tube that delivered Benadryl straight into my vein. The hives and itching stopped almost immediately.

Even if you've never had an allergic reaction, it's worth knowing how to recognize the signs. Allergies like mine can pop up at any time. Ingredients such as peanut dust can get into foods without warning, especially if factories or restaurants reuse dishes or utensils.

You might even be able to save the life of one of your friends. In one study, McMorris found that allergic kids, teenagers, and college students rarely carry epipens or tell their roommates or friends about their allergies. If you know what to look for, you can run for help in case of emergency.

- **What should a person do if he or she is having an allergic reaction? What sort of medicine would help her?**

"This is very serious business," McMorris says. "You need to respect kids with food allergies. You have to take good care of your friends."

After Reading:

- Why do you think more and more people in the United States are developing allergies?

- Develop a scale to help determine the severity of an allergic reaction.

- Make a list of at least 10 different products that have peanuts or peanut oil in them, but where peanuts are not the main ingredient. (You can go to the grocery store for further research.)

- How should a school prepare for students with severe allergies?

- The U.S. Food and Drug Administration (FDA) requires food products to carry labels that indicate whether trace amounts of peanuts may be present. Do you think this sort of food labeling is important? About what other kinds of foods should the FDA issue warnings?

- How would scientists go about creating a peanut that would be less likely to cause allergies? How would you test this new kind of peanut?

Section 2

Sports and Exercise Health

We all know it's good for our health to work out regularly or play sports. But staying physically fit isn't always easy. That's why scientists are doing research to find ways to make athletic activity safer and more fun. In this section, we look at some of the latest findings in the field of sports science.

You probably learned in gym class that it's important to stretch your muscles to get them warmed up before a workout. Interesting new studies show that this might be bad advice. As Emily Sohn explains in the first article, stretching may actually increase the risk of injury in some situations.

Certain sports with lots of physical contact, like football, can lead to cuts and bruises. Although nobody likes the pain of a scratch or scrape, these injuries seem like nothing to worry about. In the second article, however, Emily Sohn shows how getting cut while playing sports can expose you to dangerous infection and even deadly illness.

In the third article, we examine findings that show young people are particularly vulnerable to fractures, especially while playing sports. Author Emily Sohn describes what you can do to protect yourself.

If you're into running, you probably know that a good athletic shoe can help improve your performance. In fact, you may have noticed that there are different styles of sneakers for almost every kind of sport. The fourth article looks into the science of designing sneakers to make the most of a person's fitness potential.

The final article also concerns running. Recent studies have shown that some people may naturally be faster than others because of their genes. Emily Sohn describes this newfound "speed gene."

—The Editor

Should You Stretch?

Do you stretch before a big game or a workout? If you're like most people, you do. For many years, medical scientists have believed that stretching the muscles before taking part in athletic activities helps prevent injury. Now, some new research indicates that stretching might not be the best way to prepare for sports. In fact, it's even possible that stretching could *increase* the chance of injury, as Emily Sohn tells us in the next article. Please keep in mind, however, that you shouldn't necessarily stop your stretching routine just because of this new information. Always talk to your doctor and athletic coach before changing the way you exercise.

—The Editor

Workouts: Does Stretching Help?

by Emily Sohn

Before Reading:

- Describe how you would warm up before a soccer game or some other sport in which you participate.

- Why is stretching commonly considered a good idea before exercise?

Touch your toes. Reach for the sky. Twist from side to side.

If you've ever played on a sports team or gone to gym class, you probably know the drill. First, you do some warmups. Then you stretch. Exercises and activities follow. At the end of class or practice, you do more stretches.

For decades, coaches and gym teachers have insisted that stretching helps athletes perform better, suffer fewer injuries, and feel less sore the next day. From the health club to the football field to the gymnastics mat, everywhere you look, people stretch.

Now, research suggests that stretching may not do your body as much good as people thought. After reviewing more than 350 scientific studies, researchers from the

Centers for Disease Control and Prevention (CDC) found that stretching may not reduce the chance of injury.

"There's insufficient evidence to demonstrate that stretching is effective," says Stephen Thacker. He's director of the CDC's **epidemiology** program in Atlanta, Georgia.

ATHLETIC PERFORMANCE

If it's athletic performance you're after, don't expect stretching to help you run faster, jump higher, or throw a ball farther, either. Some studies show that stretching may actually slow you down, especially if you do it before you play your sport.

To top it off, it now looks as if stretching may actually make you even more likely to get hurt, says Stacy Ingraham.

Ingraham is an exercise physiologist at the University of Minnesota, Twin Cities. Her research focuses on injuries in women and girls, who tend to hurt their muscles and joints more often than men do.

"Certain athletes stretch all the time," Ingraham says. "They're the ones who usually get hurt."

- **What does Stacy Ingraham do and what is her position on stretching?**

Ingraham points to professional baseball players as an example. They all do stretches before a game, she says. Yet baseball players have one of the highest rates of injury in any sport. Minnesota Twins center fielder Torii Hunter tore his hamstring in his first game of the season.

Ingraham has coached and worked with runners, basketball players, baseball players, and football players. When she persuades them to stop stretching, she says, injury rates tend to go down.

Thacker has noticed a similar pattern. He coaches a high school girl's basketball team. During his first five years of coaching, six girls tore their **ACL**, a ligament that connects the thigh to the shin and stabilizes the knee. Three years ago, Thacker replaced stretching with specific strengthening exercises and warmup activities such as jogging and sidestepping. Since then, the team has had no ACL injuries.

• **What is the ACL?**

WORKING MUSCLES

To understand why stretching may be a bad idea, it helps to know how muscles work.

It all starts as orders from the brain. Special cells called **neurons** carry electrical messages from the brain through the nervous system to the muscles you want to activate. If you're running, your brain tells your legs to move and your arms to pump. As soon as the messages get to their targets, the muscles react. You're cruising.

Skeletal muscles are the kind that attach to bones (Figure 2.1). They do most of the work when you exercise. Skeletal muscles are made up of long, twisted cells called fibers. Proteins inside the fibers help your muscles contract and relax. These muscle movements allow you to run, jump, skip, throw a Frisbee®, swim, and more.

With exercise, muscle fibers grow and multiply. The more you work out, the stronger and bigger your muscles get.

- **Draw a picture of how a skeletal muscle works.**

When you stretch, you lengthen muscle fibers. It then takes longer for messages from the brain to travel through them. Stretched muscles also seem to be more sluggish than unstretched ones. They don't spring back as readily. And every time you stretch, you may be tearing your muscle fibers a teeny bit.

Stretching before you exercise is particularly risky, experts say, because stretched muscles are less stable. That makes it harder for them to bounce back from the jarring impact of running, jumping, or weaving around other players on a soccer field.

Instead of stretching before an activity, experts recommend warming up by starting slowly to get blood and oxygen flowing to your muscles. Warming up is also a natural way of stretching your muscles just enough to prepare them for more intense activity.

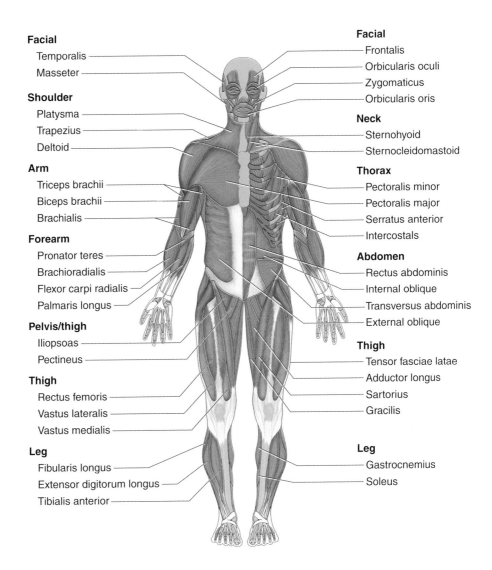

Facial
  Temporalis
  Masseter

Shoulder
  Platysma
  Trapezius
  Deltoid

Arm
  Triceps brachii
  Biceps brachii
  Brachialis

Forearm
  Pronator teres
  Brachioradialis
  Flexor carpi radialis
  Palmaris longus

Pelvis/thigh
  Iliopsoas
  Pectineus

Thigh
  Rectus femoris
  Vastus lateralis
  Vastus medialis

Leg
  Fibularis longus
  Extensor digitorum longus
  Tibialis anterior

Facial
  Frontalis
  Orbicularis oculi
  Zygomaticus
  Orbicularis oris

Neck
  Sternohyoid
  Sternocleidomastoid

Thorax
  Pectoralis minor
  Pectoralis major
  Serratus anterior
  Intercostals

Abdomen
  Rectus abdominis
  Internal oblique
  Transversus abdominis
  External oblique

Thigh
  Tensor fasciae latae
  Adductor longus
  Sartorius
  Gracilis

Leg
  Gastrocnemius
  Soleus

Figure 2.1 **The human body is made up of hundreds of muscles, which connect to bones to allow us to move.**

"If you're going to play soccer, jog a bit beforehand," Thacker says. "If you're going to play baseball, swing the bat before a game."

Kids don't get injured as often as adults do because they don't put the same kind of stresses on their joints, Thacker says. Still, it's never too early to get into good habits.

Girls, especially, have reason to worry. Among high school athletes, girls are three times more likely than boys to tear the ACL in their knees. By the time they hit the professional level, women tear their ACLs up to 10 times as often as men do, Ingraham says.

Girls hurt their ankles and backs more often than boys, too. Scientists aren't sure what causes the difference, but girls tend to be more flexible than boys, Ingraham says. Her research suggests that this extra flexibility could be part of the problem. And stretching may only make things worse.

GENTLE MOTIONS

It may be worth talking about stretching with your coaches and gym teachers.

But if they insist you keep stretching, don't be too worried, says fitness expert Jay Blahnik. He has written a book called *Full-Body Flexibility*.

In some cases, gentle stretching can be helpful,

Blahnik says, as long as you do the right kind of stretches at the right time and you do them correctly.

Instead of grabbing your ankles and yanking or forcing your body into pretzels, he suggests gentle motions that actively use your muscles.

Try clasping your hands behind your head, Blahnik recommends. Then slowly pull your elbows backward and squeeze your shoulder blades together. "The act of stretching doesn't decrease injuries," he says, "but we think being mobile and flexible does."

As part of a cooldown after a workout, light stretching is also okay, Blahnik says. And, for sports such as gymnastics and dancing, stronger stretching may be appropriate.

- **What does the article recommend an athlete do before he or she starts exercising?**

Overall, preparation for sports or exercise should involve a variety of activities, not just stretching. Athletes, coaches, trainers, and others need to use the combination of strength training, conditioning, and warming up that's best for a given sport.

Whatever you decide to do about stretching, don't stop exercising. Research continues to show that exercise is good for your heart, good for your bones, and good for your muscles. It helps you sleep better and keeps your weight under control. Running around is fun. It can even make you smarter.

Now, stop reading and get a move on!

After Reading:

- **What particular stretches would you imagine are the hardest on your body? Why?**

- **What is yoga? If you don't know, check the Internet to obtain information about yoga. See, for example, *www.americanyogaassociation.org/general.html#WhatisYoga* (*American Yoga Association*). How might yoga exercises that involve stretching help you? Could they also hurt you? Why are yoga exercises not recommended for children under 16?**

- **Why are women more flexible than men?**

- **How do supplements or diet affect how muscle fibers grow and multiply?**

- **What should an athlete do when he or she has sore muscles? See, for example, *www.kidsrunning.com/columns/coolingdowncory.html* (*KidsRunning.Com*).**

- **How does temperature affect muscles? You can learn more about muscles and how they work at *www.kidshealth.org/kid/body/muscles_noSW.html* (*KidsHealth for Kids*).**

- **How does a doctor fix a torn hamstring? See *http://orthopedics.about.com/cs/sprainsstrains/a/hamstring.htm* (*About.com*).**

Playing Sports Can Make You Sick

You probably know that taking part in sports is great exercise and that regular exercise is vital if you want to stay in shape and build strong bones and muscles. But you may not realize that sometimes, the rough and tumble of certain sports can cause more than just a little pain. As writer Emily Sohn demonstrates in the next article, recent research has shown that athletes are exposed to many types of bacteria–some of them potentially deadly–when they are injured during sporting events. Find out what to look out for and how to protect yourself while you play your favorite sport.

—The Editor

Football Scrapes and Nasty Infections

by Emily Sohn

Sports are fun, but they can also be dangerous. Broken bones, pulled muscles, and sprained joints are all common injuries among athletes. Now, researchers have identified another possible risk of playing certain sports.

Among professional football players in the United States, cuts and scrapes can lead to nasty skin infections. Caused by bacteria, many of these infections are hard to treat and resistant to common medicines.

The study focused on players for the St. Louis Rams. The team plays on a field with artificial turf instead of real grass. Scientists from the Centers for Disease Control and Prevention (CDC) in Atlanta found that, between August and November of 2003, each player averaged 2 to 3 scrapes, or turf burns, per week.

Many of these scrapes didn't just go away. Infections were common. In fact, three-fifths of the Rams players said that they had been treated with an **antibiotic** during the season. And each player received an average of 2.6 such prescriptions that year. That's 10 times the number of prescriptions that men their age who don't play professional football receive.

Out of the 58 players on the team, five developed infections that didn't improve after treatment with a few of the most common types of antibiotics. Instead, doctors had to use other types of treatment.

The infections in these five players were caused by a resistant form of a bacterium called *Staphylococcus aureus* (Figure 2.2). Staph bacteria can live harmlessly on many skin surfaces. But when the skin is punctured or broken for any reason, Staph bacteria can enter the wound and cause an infection.

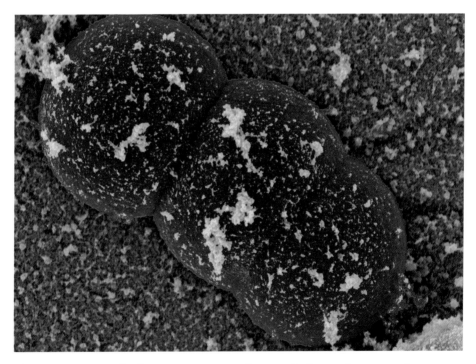

Figure 2.2 *Staphylococcus aureus* **bacteria (seen here under a microscope) cause some potentially deadly illnesses, such as toxic shock syndrome.**

During the 2003 season, some players on other teams that played against the Rams in St. Louis also suffered the same sort of infection. The CDC researchers suggest that the bacterium may get spread around during a game, going from one player's scrapes to the turf to other players' scrapes. Players can also come into contact with bacteria during practices, in locker rooms, and in the community.

Recognizing the dangers of a game doesn't mean people shouldn't play it. The new study just reinforces how important it is to take precautions. Besides wearing helmets and pads, the scientists say, football players should make sure they wash their hands a lot, shower before getting into the team's hot tubs together, and refuse to share towels.

Bruises and cuts are painful enough. Infections just add to the misery. They're another unnecessary obstacle to performing well.

Going Deeper:

Seppa, Nathan. "There's the Rub: Football Abrasions Can Lead to Nasty Infections." *Science News* 167 (February 5, 2005): 85–86. Available online at *http://www.sciencenews.org/articles/20050205/fob5.asp*.

You can learn more about infections caused by *Staphylococcus aureus* online at *http://vm.cfsan.fda.gov/~mow/chap3.html* and *http://kidshealth.org/parent/infections/bacterial_viral/staphylococcus.html*.

More Frequent Fractures

If you're like many young adults, you may have broken a
bone at some point in your life. If so, you most likely did
it while taking part in some kind of athletic activity, like
bicycling, skateboarding, or playing a contact sport. In
fact, the latest scientific data show that youth—especially between the ages of 10 and 16—is the most common
time for people to suffer bone fractures. In the following
article, writer Emily Sohn analyzes the reasons behind
this phenomenon and explains the steps you can take to
avoid being part of the growing number of young people
with broken bones.

—The Editor

Prime Time for Broken Bones

by Emily Sohn

Kids will be kids. They climb trees. They ride skateboards down steps. They jump off swing-sets. No matter how often adults warn them to be careful, accidents occur and bones break. That's happened generation after generation.

There's a new reason now to pay attention to warnings, however. A recent study found that young people today are breaking their forearms far more often than kids did just 30 years ago.

Researchers from the Mayo Clinic in Rochester, Minnesota, looked at medical records from the Rochester area during two three-year blocks: 1968–1971 and 1998–2001. Overall, there were 42% more forearm fractures during the more recent period. The study included people up to age 35, but most breaks happened between ages 10 and 16.

Breaks during sports and other recreational activities increased the most, doubling over the 30-year period. In males, there was a sharp increase in fracture-inducing accidents during inline skating, skateboarding, skiing, hockey, and bicycling. Females broke significantly more bones from skating, skiing, soccer, and basketball.

Kids might be more active than they used to be, which is one possible explanation for the trend. Diet could be another reason. More young people today drink soda and sweetened juices instead of calcium-rich milk. Calcium helps build strong bones.

At the same time, the inactive lifestyle of some kids may also contribute to the problem. Today's kids may be more out of shape from too much time spent playing video games, watching TV, and snacking. When they go out to play, they may be more likely to fall and break a limb.

So, when you go out to play, consider wearing a helmet and other protective gear. At dinner, make sure you eat enough calcium. And it might make sense to listen to adults when they tell you to watch out.

Going Deeper:

Raloff, Janet. "The Risks in Sweet Solutions to Young Thirsts." *Science News Online* (September 27, 2003). Available online at *http://www.sciencenews.org/20030927/food.asp*.

Seppa, Nathan. "Broken Arms Way up." *Science News* 164(October 4, 2003): 221. Available online at *http://www.sciencenews.org/20031004/note13.asp*.

You can learn the facts about broken bones online at *www.kidshealth.org/kid/ill_injure/aches/broken_bones.html*.

Sophisticated Shoes for Sports

If you've ever been to an athletic footwear store, you already know that sneakers come in lots of varieties. There seems to be a special shoe for every possible sport, from walking to tennis to cross-training. How do scientists figure out what kind of shoe works best for each different sport? You may be surprised to learn that an entire field of science deals with matching human anatomy to appropriate footwear: sneaker science. In the following article, writer Emily Sohn takes a look at the exciting field of sports footwear development.

–The Editor

Running With Sneaker Science

by Emily Sohn

Before Reading:

- When you decide to buy new sneakers, what are the most important features you look for?

- Why are basketball sneakers usually made of leather?

- What would you do to prepare to run a marathon?

At mile 12, my feet were already starting to hurt. By mile 17 of the 2003 Boston marathon, I was over-whelmed by an urge to stop. The muscles in my thighs were cramping up. My back ached. The soles of my feet throbbed. I felt as if I had been hit by a truck. There were still 9 hilly miles to go.

From that point on, the intense highs and lows of long-distance running consumed me. During some stretches, I thought I might just crumple to the ground. Then, inspired by the roaring crowd, my stride would suddenly feel strong and smooth. My body would become a machine, light as a feather.

The joy of completing my second marathon carried

Figure 2.3 Sneaker science focuses on the development of special shoes to help you excel in your favorite sport.

me across the finish line 3 hours, 40 minutes, and 16 seconds after I had begun. Agony immediately took over. I couldn't walk properly for days.

All of the excitement over the New York City marathon, run six months after Boston on November 2, 2003, inspired a new wave of marathon fever in me. I've already talked with a few friends about running it together next year. At the same time, I have mixed feelings about how much more my body can take. I just ran my third marathon a month ago. Now, I can't run a step, due to a deeply cracked shin bone that is also keeping me from doing many of the other things I love, like climbing, biking, even walking and yoga.

A distance of 26.2 miles [42.2 km] is just a long way to run, says Seth Kinley, an athletic trainer at Pennsylvania State University in University Park, Pennsylvania. "The bottom of your foot strikes the ground thousands of times."

In labs across the country, researchers are using high-tech equipment to design new kinds of gear and improve training routines. By addressing nagging pains and other problems, sneaker science is helping athletes go faster, stronger, and longer (Figure 2.3).

DESIGNING BETTER GEAR

To combat the stresses inflicted by running and other sports, scientists study how the body moves. They then search for ways to help it move better.

Improvements often happen in baby steps. It can take as long as two years to turn an idea into a shoe that you can buy in a store, says Gordon Valiant, a biomechanist at Nike headquarters in Beaverton, Oregon.

The process begins when an athlete or employee points out a specific need. Some athletes might want a shoe that prevents knee injuries. Others might wish to sprint faster or get a quicker start. Still others might want a shoe that works well on mountain trails.

NEWS DETECTIVE   by Emily Sohn

Sports have always been a big part of my life. I was a dedicated member of my high school varsity soccer, swimming, and lacrosse teams. As a senior, I co-captained the girl's soccer and coed swim teams. When I got to college, I swam on the women's varsity swim team for a year, before moving on to ultimate Frisbee®, which didn't require quite as intense a commitment.

Until I stopped swimming, practices structured my life. I loved setting goals, training with a purpose, measuring improvements, feeling strong and fast, and working with a team. Most of my best friends were also teammates.

Still, I never thought I'd end up running marathons. I was a distance swimmer and an avid hiker. In those activities, I could happily go for hours without stopping. But I used to hate running for its own sake. After a few miles, I'd end up bored and exhausted.

When I left college and started moving a lot, I found that running was one kind of exercise I could do anywhere. Funny enough, the more running I did, the more I actually enjoyed it.

Soon after moving to Minnesota, I met my friend Annie. She had already run four marathons and had vowed to keep running them until she qualified for Boston. Her best time, 3 hours and 42 minutes, was still 2 minutes shy of the 3:40 qualifying time for our age group. She was looking for a training partner, she told me when we first met. Was I interested?

That was nearly two years ago. Months of running together has turned Annie into one of my best friends. We talk about everything on our long training runs, bonded by foul weather and strange pains.

Annie and I ran Grandma's Marathon in Duluth, Minnesota, in June 2002. Even though it was my first running race ever, both of us managed to qualify for Boston! I finished in 3 hours, 37 minutes. Annie squeezed in at 3 hours, 39 minutes.

Boston was a tougher course than Grandma's. The physical and mental anguish was intense. Still, nothing can compare to the feeling of finishing a marathon after months of training. And, as painful as it is to run 26.2 consecutive miles, there is something addictive about the sense of accomplishment.

In fact, I signed up for the Twin Cities Marathon just weeks after finishing Boston, even though I vowed that it, too, would be my last one. I ran my best time yet: 3:34. Now I'm injured and can't run at all. Perhaps, it's time to retire from marathons once and for all. Or maybe, once I recover, I'll do just one more. . . .

Experiments come next. At the Nike Sports Research Lab in Beaverton, basketball courts, treadmills, and padded running platforms have sensors that measure the forces of impact. Wind tunnels and temperature-controlled chambers simulate real-world conditions. High-speed cameras take a thousand or more pictures per second. Computers perform analyses. Athletes come in to run and jump. A team of more than 25 experts watches their every move.

- **How is a wind tunnel a useful tool for scientists studying the performance of a sneaker?**

"We spend a lot of time in the lab measuring the different forces acting on the lower extremities and feet of athletes," Valiant says. "That gives us insight into how we can either enhance or not interfere with the athlete's motion, while at the same time protecting them from forces, or allowing them to use forces to their advantage. Knowledge of those things can really be applied to innovative designs."

Adidas, New Balance, Reebok, and other companies conduct their own research, all with the same goal–to make better, faster, cooler-looking shoes. Of course, profits are important, too. Sneakers, as you may know, can cost a lot of money, and the market is extremely competitive. Research is also going on at universities, sometimes for commercial reasons, other times to help

Scientist's Notebook by Emily Sohn

Sneaker scientists and sports trainers spend so much time analyzing how athletes move, you would think they'd have to be sports nuts themselves. For the most part, that's true.

"On staff here at Nike, we have basketball players, lots of runners, soccer players, football players, golfers," says Nike biomechanist Gordon Valiant. "We're all active and interested in sports."

In fact, an interest in sports motivated many of Nike's experts to go into the field in the first place. "It's a very fun place to work," Valiant says. "It's actually pretty cool to go through university and study something you're interested in and then apply it to something you're interested in."

Being around so many athletes and constantly working to create better gear also seems to give Nike's staff the urge to go, go, go. Business director Mark Riley and communications manager Beth Hegde have each run many marathons. This year, Mark decided at the last minute to run his 12th Boston marathon, while Beth chose to take a break from the race.

"Sometimes, we'll decide the day before a marathon to run it," Mark told me, "usually just for fun."

Seth Kinley, a trainer at Penn State, has a different perspective. After treating runners' injuries for 10 years, he has learned the importance of rest for both health and performance.

"These kids live, breathe, and will probably die running," he says. "I try to get through to them that they will be better off if they take some time off."

Kinley takes his own advice seriously. He has run a few 5-kilometer [3-mile] races, but that's about it. "I'm not much of a runner," he says.

coaches and athletes train better, or simply for the scientific interest of the work.

BASIC MOVEMENTS

The basic movement of a runner's foot is fairly simple. The heel strikes the ground first, followed by a roll inward toward the toes. Then, the foot goes rigid, which allows the runner to launch forward, in a springboard kind of way. Any slight variation in that ideal running form can end up causing all sorts of injuries.

"Pain in the knees, hips, and back can all stem from what's going on in the foot," says Kinley, who has worked with runners at Penn State for 10 years.

Everyone's feet are different, though there are some general categories based on the shape of the arch. I have slightly flat feet, which makes my legs roll inward and throws my stride off kilter. I used to have severe knee pain as a result, until I started wearing stable shoes with lots of support.

> • Why can jogging, or even walking, with the wrong kind of shoes contribute to a knee injury?

Each shoe and piece of clothing is designed and tested to meet specific needs, Valiant says.

Marathon runners want lightweight footwear with plenty of cushioning, for example. Racing shoes for shorter distances often sacrifice cushioning for flexibility. Basketball shoes need to be sturdy enough to deal with lots of twisting and jumping.

Moreover, the best combination of shoe length and width varies from men to women to kids, and among people from different ethnic backgrounds.

With so many choices, it's important to make sure you don't get sucked in by the latest styles, Kinley says. "Just because it's fancier looking or has cool colors or costs a lot," he says, "doesn't mean it's a better shoe to have."

- **What is the most crucial quality to look for if you need a good pair of sneakers to run the 100-meter dash? How do those sneakers compare with those needed to play tennis?**

MARATHON TIPS

Hoping to avoid some of the pain of my first marathon, which I had run months before in Minnesota, I went looking for tips at the Nike store in Boston the day before the 2003 race. There, I met Mark Riley, business director for men's running footwear. He had traveled from Nike headquarters to run his 12th Boston marathon.

Mark showed me some of Nike's newest products. He didn't seem to

- **Why does Seth Kinley think style should not be your first priority when choosing what to wear on your feet?**

mind that I was wearing New Balance shoes. Then, talk turned to race-day strategies.

"Don't start out too fast," Mark warned me over and over. The biggest hills come late in the race, he said, and you want to make sure you have enough energy left to charge up the slopes. "Trust your training," he added. "You'll do great."

Of course, when it comes to running marathons, anything can happen. On April 21, 2003, in Boston, temperatures soared to 75 degrees [24°C] under a fierce sun. A strong head wind blew for the last 10 miles [16 km] of the race.

When I finally reached the end, I realized that no amount of sneaker science could have kept my feet from aching, along with my legs, back, lungs, and everything else. When it comes to a marathon, shoes do matter. But determination matters more.

After Reading:

- What are some major differences between the footwear needs of a woman and of a man?

- If you wanted to buy your grandmother a pair of shoes for her birthday, what kind would you get her? Why?

- Scientists use treadmills and other types of equipment to study and compare sneakers. If you were a scientist and wanted to study the performance of several different automobiles, what kinds of equipment would you need in your laboratory?

- Along with shoes, what clothing is important for a runner's performance? What issues should be taken into account when designing shirts and pants for runners?

Is Speed in Your Genes?

It's an obvious fact that some people run or skate faster than others. But what gives these people the speedy edge? Is it their body shape? Their training? Their weight? According to recent research, speed may actually be genetic. As author Emily Sohn explains in the next article, scientists have discovered that certain "high-speed" athletes are more likely to have a particular gene in their bodies, which may play a role in giving them a competitive edge.

—The Editor

Speedy Gene Gives Runners a Boost

by Emily Sohn

No matter how hard you push yourself, you probably still can't run as fast as some of your friends. Even with tons of training, most of us could never be Olympians.

In fact, if you watch elite sprinters in action, you might think they are just born with something the rest of us don't have. Now, new research suggests what that might be.

Speedy runners are more likely to have a certain gene than other people, say scientists in Australia. The gene tells the body to make a protein called **alpha-actinin-3**. This protein works in **fast-twitch muscles**, which provide bursts of power for activities like sprinting or speed skating.

Kathryn North of Children's Hospital at Westmead in Sydney, Australia, and her colleagues thought the protein might affect sprinting speed. So, the researchers compared star sprinters to endurance athletes and other people.

In their study, 94% of sprinters and speed skaters had the gene for making alpha-actinin-3. In comparison, only 82% of nonathletes had it. And 76% of marathon runners and other endurance athletes had it.

Alpha-actinin-3 might give sprinters an extra boost when they need it. And North suggests that not having the protein might help endurance athletes stay strong during lengthy exertion.

The research may eventually help explain why some people are so much faster than others.

But even if you aren't biologically destined to break records at the 100-meter dash, keep practicing your stride. There might be marathons in your future!

Going Deeper:

McDonagh, Sorcha. "Turbo Gene: Getting a Speed Boost From DNA." *Science News* 164 (August 2, 2003): 70. Available online at *http://www.sciencenews.org/20030802/fob7.asp*.

Section 3

The Science of
Good Health

Every day, we are bombarded by new information about what we need to do to stay healthy. We are told to eat a balanced diet (which seems to mean something different to every different "expert"), we are told to exercise regularly, and we are reminded to always get plenty of sleep. Health science is a field that grows and changes with almost every passing minute. In this section, we look at some of the latest trends and research into the science of living better.

The first article examines the importance of strong bones. From the dangers of broken bones to the long-term problem of osteoporosis, there are many reasons to be concerned about your skeletal system, since it forms the structure and support for your entire body.

The second article focuses on the "germs" that live in our guts. It may sound gross to think about foreign organisms living inside our bodies, but the fact is, there are many kinds of bacteria that make their homes in your stomach and digestive tract. These helpful bacteria play a major role in keeping you healthy.

The third article takes a look at a topic you've probably heard about a lot: sleep. Everyone's heard that you should try to get about eight hours of sleep each night. You probably even know something about the different stages of sleep and the importance of getting "high-quality" rest. But did you know that sleeping soundly can actually help you live longer? Writer Emily Sohn explains some fascinating new research that relates the quality of sleep you get to how long you may live.

The last article is about an unusual topic: caring for other people. At first glance, this may not seem like a health issue, but scientists have shown that the more people care about others, the more likely they are to live long and healthy lives.

—The Editor

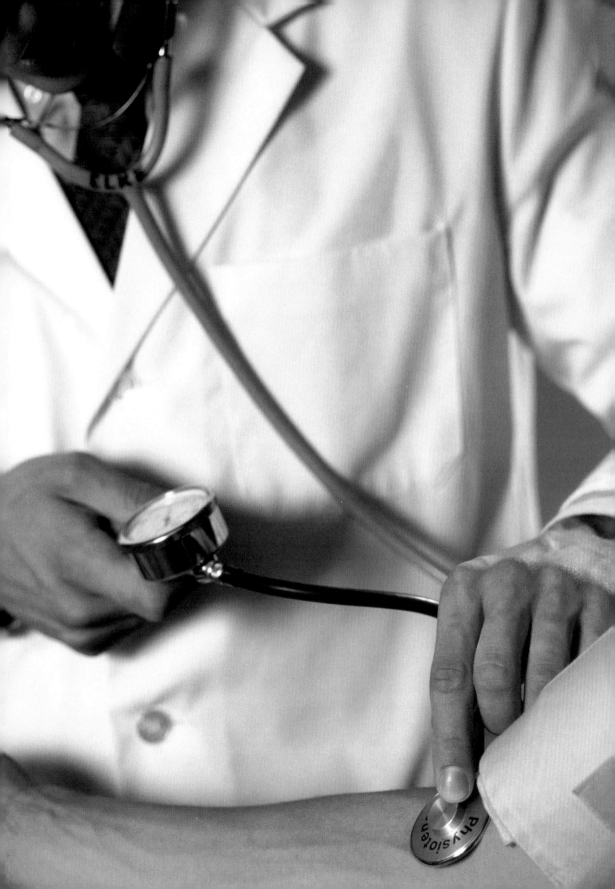

Build Better Bones

When you think of bones, what comes to mind? If you said a hard texture, you're not alone. Most people picture their bones as almost rock-hard structures. In fact, however, bones are extremely porous—they have tons of tiny holes and tunnels. This amazing design allows bones to be both strong and sturdy for holding up your body and light enough for you to carry around without getting too tired! Although you may not think about caring for your bones often—after all, only old people get stooped over and break their hips, right?—the time to build healthy bones is while you are still young. In the next article, writer Emily Sohn explains the best ways to do just that.

—The Editor

Strong Bones for Life

by Emily Sohn

Before Reading:

- **What do you think could happen if you don't take care of your bones?**

- **What sort of nutrition is important for kids to make sure they develop strong bones?**

If you're like most kids, you probably think you'll never get old. Achy joints, failing eyesight, heart attacks: These are things you won't have to deal with for a long time, right? So why worry now?

As it turns out, the choices you make now can make a big difference in how you feel later in life. I recently learned this lesson the hard way.

It started with an injury: a cracked shinbone caused by too much running on hard pavement. My doctor suggested a bone scan, which showed that my bones are weaker than average. I don't have **osteoporosis**, a disease that causes older people to shrink in height and break bones easily. But I'm close.

For me, the diagnosis was a scary wakeup call. I'm just

27 years old, but already I'm worried about things that normally happen only to women more than twice my age. Will I break my hip if I slip on a patch of ice? Is it safe for me to go skiing, lift heavy boxes, play Ultimate Frisbee®?

Perhaps what upsets me most is the realization that I might have avoided all of this if only I had thought ahead earlier in life. Childhood and adolescence are the most important times to build strong bones. For you, there's still time. Doctors suggest a variety of foods you can eat and exercises you can do as a teenager to build strong bones for life.

LIVING TISSUE

Bones are amazing. They're hard but flexible, and they're lightweight but tough. Without bones, we'd be just puddles of skin and guts.

An adult person has 206 bones in his or her body. The outer layer of a typical bone is made of a hard material honeycombed with tunnels. This web of hollow pipes allows a bone to be strong and light. It also allows the passage of nutrients and waste. A protein called collagen gives a bone its elasticity. Chemicals known as calcium salts make a bone hard.

But, even though our bones support us, they're easy to ignore. Unlike a cut or bruise, a weak bone isn't visible or painful.

Osteoporosis is sometimes called a silent disease. People often don't realize they have it until it has progressed so far that they break bones while doing ordinary things, such as walking down stairs or lifting heavy objects.

Osteoporosis happens mostly to older people. But I'm not the only woman in her 20s with weak bones. Increasingly, scientists are finding that weak bones are a problem in teenagers and even younger kids. That's especially troubling because youth is the critical time for bone growth.

If you've ever seen a skeleton in a museum, you might think that bones are dead. In fact, bones are living tissue. They reshape and rebuild themselves many times as you grow and age.

- **What is osteoporosis? How can you tell if you suffer from osteoporosis?**

The cycle of building and breaking down bone changes over a person's lifetime. Bone-building is fastest during the first three years of life and again during adolescence. By the time you're in your 20s, the tissue in your bones is about as tightly packed as it's going to get.

Measuring something called bone density tells you how tightly packed the bone tissue is. A high bone density normally shows that you have strong bones.

Once you get to be about 35 years old, bone tissue

gets broken down more quickly than it's replaced. This means that bones tend to lose tissue, and the bone density goes down. That's when osteoporosis usually becomes a concern. And it's a bigger risk for women than for men.

FOOD CONCERNS

Getting the right kind of bone-building nutrition and exercise as a teenager is like putting money in the bank. Your bones can stay strong as you get older.

Unfortunately, many teenagers don't think about their bones when they order lunch or decide what to do with their free time. They'd rather snack on chips or slurp soda than think about vitamins.

And parents don't always set the best example. "I was standing by the elevator at Children's Hospital," says Susan Coupey, an adolescent medical specialist at Children's Hospital at Montefiore in Bronx, New York. "There was a two-year-old child being fed soda by his parents."

Junk food has few nutrients. It also fills you up, so you don't eat enough of the good stuff. That's one reason why many adults want schools to get rid of soda machines.

Doctors urge kids to get plenty of calcium, the mineral that makes bones strong. Calcium is also essential for keeping nerves, blood, and muscles healthy. When you don't take in enough calcium, your body takes calcium out of your bones, which weakens your bones even more.

Although calcium is abundant in milk, yogurt, cheese, fortified juices, soy milk, and some nuts and vegetables, few people get enough of it. The Institute of Medicine recommends that kids between the ages of 9 and 18 get 1,300 milligrams of calcium every day. That's roughly the amount of calcium in a quart of milk.

Yet fewer than 10% of girls and 25% of boys get that much, according to the National Osteoporosis Foundation. "The average calcium intake of adolescent girls in the

• **What role does calcium play in bones?**

United States is somewhere around 900 milligrams," Coupey says. "Many take in just 600 to 700 milligrams."

PAYING ATTENTION

Now that I've started paying attention, I realize that getting enough calcium takes some effort (Figure 3.1). Getting 1,300 milligrams of calcium is equivalent to drinking about 4 glasses of milk, eating 10 cups of cooked broccoli, or having 2 glasses of milk, a cup of yogurt, and a glass of orange juice–every day!

And that's not all you need. To absorb the calcium you eat, you have to take in a variety of other vitamins and minerals, including lots of vitamin D.

In the summertime, you get vitamin D from sunlight on your skin. Where I live in Minnesota, though, it's too

Figure 3.1 **Getting plenty of calcium in your diet is one of the best ways to build strong bones. All of these foods are good sources of calcium.**

dark and cold much of the year to spend a great deal of time outside. To get the recommended 400 to 800 international units of vitamin D recommended for people my age, I drink 2 cups of fortified milk every day, and I take a vitamin supplement. The American Academy of Pediatrics now recommends that teenagers take a daily multivitamin that has 200 international units of vitamin D.

Getting enough exercise is also crucial. "There have been some really excellent studies showing the effectiveness of weight-bearing exercise and strengthening exercises on bone density," Coupey says.

Any exercise at all is better than sitting in front of the TV. Walking and lifting weights, in particular, are great for building muscles that support and strengthen bone. Playing soccer, tennis, or basketball are also good options.

A recent study found that elementary school girls who did jumping exercises for 10 to 12 minutes, three times a week, built 5 percent more bone mass than did girls who didn't do the exercises. That's enough bone mass to buy women some extra bone strength later in life, said the scientists from the University of British Columbia who did the study.

Even if you're glued to the TV set, why not do some jumping jacks during the commercials? Have a glass of milk or fortified juice and some almonds instead of a can of soda and chips.

• **Besides changing your diet to include more calcium, what else can you do to strengthen your bones?**

The changes are small, but the payoff could be big. You might even be amazed at how good it feels to take care of your bones. Support them, and they will support you for many years to come.

After Reading:

• Given the suggestions provided in this article for protecting and increasing the health of your bones, do you think you're doing a better or worse job than most of your classmates? Why?

• Do you think there should be soda machines in schools? Why or why not?

• What suggestions would you offer to a friend who wants to protect her bones but is allergic to milk products?

• How do bones change over time?

• Create a three-day menu of meals (breakfast, lunch, and dinner) that would help prevent bone weakness.

• Coupey suggests that people do "weight-bearing exercise and strengthening exercises." Name three sports in which players would get such exercise.

Helpful Germs

The word *bacteria* usually makes you think of dangerous, even deadly infections like *E. coli* or *Streptococcus*. But did you know that right now there are millions, even billions, of helpful bacteria living inside your stomach? It's true, and it's a win-win situation. The bacteria get a warm, cozy place to live, while in return, you get protection against potentially harmful types of bacteria and other organisms. Find out about the cooperative relationship we all share with these microscopic helpers.

—The Editor

Gut Germs to the Rescue

by Emily Sohn

In many situations, bacteria are bad guys. As soon as your defenses are down, the tiny microbes infect your body and make you sick.

Germs can also be good for you, researchers are discovering. Between 500 and 1,000 different kinds of microbes live in a person's intestines. There are, in fact, more bacteria in your gut than cells in your entire body. Many of them may help keep us healthy.

Take *Bacteroides thetaiotaomicron*, for example. The tiny bacterium lives in our intestines and feeds off the food we eat. In exchange, *B. thetaiotaomicron* helps break down indigestible nuggets of food into sugars and produce vitamins that we can use.

The wonders of gut microbes don't stop there. *B. thetaiotaomicron* also seems to regulate specific genes in the gut and helps the intestines work better by sparking the growth of blood vessels. This "good" bacterium even stimulates the production of a chemical that kills other kinds of "bad," disease-causing bacteria.

To study how bacteria cause disease, scientists have created mice that have no germs at all. These animals end up needing to eat much more than do normal rodents, and they are much more likely to get sick.

By introducing just *B. thetaiotaomicron* into germ-free mice, researchers can find out what changes these particular bacteria cause. These changes include altering which sugars the intestine makes and keeping gut bacteria from sneaking into other parts of the body.

As more details emerge about how important gut bacteria are to our health, you might want to add a Bacteria Appreciation Day to your datebook!

Going Deeper:

Travis, John. "Gut Check." *Science News* 163 (May 31, 2003): 344–345. Available online at *http://www.sciencenews.org/20030531/bob9.asp*.

Sleep Well, Live Longer

You know how sluggish you feel when you don't get enough sleep. You can't concentrate and you may get irritated at your friends and family. But, as Emily Sohn explains in the following article, not getting enough sleep may not just be an inconvenience. Some scientists believe it may *kill* you!

—The Editor

Sleeping Soundly for a Longer Life

by Emily Sohn

You've heard it before: If you know what's good for you, you'll go to bed on time. Now, scientists are saying something more about going to sleep. And you may lose more than just TV privileges if you don't listen. You might end up shaving years off your life.

For 19 years, psychologist Mary A. Dew of the University of Pittsburgh School of Medicine and her colleagues tracked 186 healthy elderly adults, who were mostly between 60 and 80 years old. Part of the research involved monitoring brain waves of the people as they slept.

At the end of the study, the people who had trouble falling or staying asleep were more likely to die sooner from natural causes compared to those who slept well, the researchers reported.

Scientists aren't yet sure why losing sleep might shorten lives. Some experts think sleep deprivation weakens the immune system, making it harder to fight off illnesses. Other studies have linked sleep disorders to heart and brain diseases.

The new study focused on older people. But there may be a lesson here for all of us: Work hard, play hard, sleep well. You just might wake up to a longer future.

Going Deeper:

Bower, Bruce. "Bad Sleepers Hurry Death: Snoozing Soundly Staves off the Big Sleep." *Science News* 163(February 8, 2003): 85. Available online at *http://www.sciencenews.org/20030208/fob4.asp*.

Romanek, Trudee. *Zzz. . . .: The Most Interesting Book You'll Ever Read About Sleep*. Toronto, Ontario: Kids Can Press, 2002.

New Reasons to Be Nice

We all know it's "nice" to help other people, but scientists are now showing that there may be some reasons beyond good manners to try to care more about others. According to new research, as people get older, they may be able to live longer if they stay active by helping to care for friends and family, .

—The Editor

Seniors Who Care Live Longer

by Emily Sohn

Be nice. Your life might just depend on it.

Older people who took care of others lived longer than seniors who were less helpful, a recent study found. It was one of the first inquiries to focus on people who give care rather than get it.

The study, which began in 1987, surveyed 423 married couples living near Detroit. At the beginning of the project, husbands were all 65 years of age or older. Wives were slightly younger. After 5 years, 134 participants had died.

When researchers from the University of Michigan in Ann Arbor recently looked at surveys taken during the study, they found some interesting patterns.

Participants were half as likely to die during the course of the study if they regularly helped friends, relatives, and neighbors with tasks like errands and housework. People who listened closely and lovingly to their husbands and wives survived longer, too.

It's not clear whether being helpful led to a longer life or whether healthier people were more likely to offer help.

Still, it might make sense to get in the habit of helping others. It may be best for you, too, in the long run.

Going Deeper:

Bower, Bruce. "Giving Aid, Staying Alive: Elderly Helpers Have Longevity Advantage." *Science News* 164 (July 26, 2003): 51–52. Available online at *http://www.sciencenews.org/ 20030726/fob2.asp*.

Section 4

New Research in Health and Medicine

Scientists are always working to find ways to help us live longer, healthier, happier lives. In this section, we look at some of the latest research in the field of health science.

The first article looks at the growing science of seeking "natural" cures for disease. According to new research, herbs and even the slimy residue produced by certain animals and plants may have valuable uses in medicine.

The second article discusses the possible uses of electricity in treating or even curing some of the world's most devastating diseases. By utilizing the way the human brain conducts electrical signals to carry out its functions, doctors may soon have new options for treating serious illnesses.

In the third article, writer Emily Sohn examines the controversy over cell phones and whether they may be hazardous to your health. Although scientists still disagree on the dangers cell phones pose for the brain, Sohn raises some issues that are worth considering before you make your next call.

You may have heard of the exciting new field called "nanoscience," which uses tiny tools improve everything from computers to MP3 players. Sorcha McDonagh shows how tiny microchips may be able to deliver doses of medication from right inside the patient's body. The photo on the opposite page shows an artist's depiction of this new technique.

The fifth article looks at the shocking notion of using tapeworms to provide people with healing drugs, while the sixth article examines "buckyballs"—strange, multi-sided molecules that may be harmful to living cells but may also be able to help fight disease.

Finally, we revisit the issue of bones—something that can't be overemphasized when it comes to the science of health.

—The Editor

Finding Cures in Nature

You've probably never been stung by a stingray, and most likely, that's for the best. But according to new research, the mucus of a stingray might actually be helpful if you get a bad scrape on your leg. Scientists have found that the natural mucus a stingray produces may be a great infection fighter. Similar results have been found for countless plants, too. In fact, the business of finding helpful cures in nature is booming.

—The Editor

Nature's Medicines

by Emily Sohn

Before Reading:

- **How would you define what a "natural" medicine is?**

- **What did people do to ease pain or treat headaches before aspirin, Advil®, or Tylenol®?**

You would probably never think to slap a stingray on a scraped knee. Eighteen-year-old Ben Powell, however, has found compounds on a stingray's skin that may help fight infections.

Several clues had pointed to the possibility that there might be something special about stingray skin. Atlantic stingrays, for example, can deal with microbes in both fresh water and seawater. Sharks, which have a similar type of skin, sometimes nibble on each other but don't appear to get skin infections.

"I figured something had to be going on," Ben says. He's a senior at Sarasota High School in Sarasota, Florida.

Ben presented his research results in April 2005 at the

2005 Intel International Science and Engineering Fair (ISEF) in Phoenix, Arizona. He was one of a record 1,447 high school students from 45 countries who participated in the fair. The young scientists competed for more than $3 million in scholarships, trips, and other prizes.

SLIMY STUFF

Ben's project was one of several at ISEF that focused on medical treatments that may be lurking in nature.

- **Why did Ben Powell hypothesize that chemicals in a stingray's skin might fight infection?**

- **What does ISEF stand for? Who participates in this competition?**

An internship at Mote Marine Laboratory near his home inspired Ben's interest in stingrays. When he started working there in 2003, he spent most of his time feeding the aquarium's sharks, skates, and stingrays.

Eventually, Ben started talking to doctors at the lab. They were conducting medical research on the animals. Among the things that Ben learned was that young trout and salmon produce chemicals that appear to fight cancer.

Ben wondered whether stingrays might also produce chemicals that have a beneficial effect. He had noticed that stingrays rarely get sick, even though they live in an environment full of disease-causing bacteria. He hypothesized that stingrays might have microbe-fighting powers.

To test his idea, Ben studied mucus that had been scraped off the skin of stingrays living at the aquarium. Through a series of experiments, he discovered several proteins in the mucus that killed bacteria.

In the summer of 2005, Ben planned to see whether a stingray's mucous proteins can kill bacteria among a mammal's blood cells. The ultimate goal would be to copy stingray biology to produce new types of antibiotic medicines for people.

DOWN WITH SWELLING

The idea that stingray mucus could harbor medicine may sound unusual, but pursuing unusual ideas is one mark of a successful researcher, says Kels Phelps. He's a 17-year-old junior at Butte High School in Butte, Montana.

"In the search for new medicines," Kels says, "it's important to cover all the bases." Like Ben, Kels found a possible source for medicine not in a drugstore, but in nature.

For his project, Kels studied a plant called *Yucca glauca*, which grows naturally in Montana. The Cheyenne Indians have long used yucca plants as medicine. They believe yucca reduces inflammation, or swelling, just as Advil®, Aleve®, and other common medications do. Kels was interested in investigating the chemistry behind the Indian claim.

- **Why was Kels Phelps interested in the soapweed yucca plant?**

Inflammation is what happens to your ankle after you twist it or to your arm after an allergic reaction to a bee sting. You probably feel pain and notice puffiness in the area of the injury. These signs of injury typically go away after a few days.

Inflammation that doesn't go away is a major cause of discomfort and complications in a number of serious diseases, including multiple sclerosis (MS), arthritis, and Huntington's disease. In these cases, certain **enzymes** in the body become overactive and cause excessive inflammation.

- **When can inflammation occur? What are its main symptoms?**

Kels began by separating yucca plants into their parts: roots, stems, and flowers. He soaked the parts in a special solution. Then, he extracted promising chemical compounds from the mixtures. His lab experiments showed that these compounds were good at fighting certain types of microbes.

"I took a step toward proving that yucca has anti-inflammatory properties," Kels says. His work also showed him how much nature has to offer and how little we know about the world around us.

"As far as the vast number of plants out there and the

small amount of research done on them," he says, "there's a huge, untapped resource for the next generation of medicines."

GREEN TEA

Iddoshe Hirpa tapped into this enormous resource for her project on green tea. She had heard about possible health benefits and anticancer properties of the green tea plant (called *Camellia sinensis*), and she wanted to learn more.

"Both my parents are from Africa," says the 15-year-old 10th grader from duPont Manual Magnet High School in Louisville, Kentucky. "People there don't have access to all the medicines we have here."

Iddoshe worked with a chemical called **EGCG**, which occurs naturally in green tea. Past research had suggested that EGCG fights inflammation.

For her experiments, Iddoshe applied three different concentrations of EGCG to proteins that cause inflammation in the brains of people who suffer from MS. She found that the highest concentration of EGCG she used destroyed the most proteins. This result confirms, she says, that green tea really can reduce inflammation.

Iddoshe was so impressed by her results that she started buying and

- **Explain why the compound EGCG was important to Iddoshe's project. See** *www.msnbc.msn.com/id/7187847/.*

drinking green tea (which she loads with milk and sugar to make it taste good). Lately, though, she's fallen out of the habit. "I feel even worse now because I know how good it is for you," she says. "It's so embarrassing."

Even as Iddoshe struggles to make green tea part of her daily routine, she has learned an important lesson from her work.

"It's a wakeup call to people," she says. The more we destroy nature, the more we destroy possibilities for healing our own problems. "There are so many things nature could give us."

• **What made Iddoshe Hirpa start drinking lots of green tea?**

ACHIEVEMENTS

ISEF projects show just how much students can achieve when they pursue a passion, says Intel's Craig Barrett. Intel sponsored the competition along with more than 70 other organizations, government agencies, universities, and corporations.

"I have faith this new generation of young scientists and engineers will help cure diseases, protect the environment, and develop breakthrough technologies that will one day change the world," Barrett says.

If Ben, Kels, and Iddoshe are any indication, the next generation is already partway there.

After Reading:

- What medicines that are not prescribed by a doctor do you use? Are any of these "natural" medicines? If so, why do you use them?

- Why are some researchers and doctors interested in folk or herbal medicines?

- Of the three science projects described in the article, which one do you think has the most benefit for society? Why?

- Come up with three reasons why it might be important to have alternatives to modern painkillers such as Advil® or Tylenol®?

- If you were a judge at the Intel International Science and Engineering Fair and you had to judge the three projects described in the article, what questions would you ask each student? How would you decide which project is the best of the three?

An Electrical Cure

All of our bodies are filled with electricity. That might sound strange, but it's true. The signals your brain sends to your limbs and that your brain gets from your senses are all conducted by electrical sparks. Because of this simple fact, scientists have discovered that it may be possible to use electricity to help "rewire" the body when it stops functioning correctly. In fact, "electrical cures" are in the works for all kinds of illnesses, from paralyzed muscles to the tremors of Parkinson's disease.

—The Editor

Electricity's Spark of Life

by Emily Sohn

Before Reading:

- **When do we actually get to see electricity?**

- **What are the most important things we power with electricity? What would you miss the most if your electric power were to fail?**

Lots of kids get scared when their bedroom lights go out at night. When an entire city goes dark, many more people start to worry.

Government and utility officials are still scrambling to explain a blackout that hit much of the northeastern United States in the late summer of 2003. From Detroit to New York, lights went out. Refrigerators, traffic signals, elevators, and subway trains stopped working. Computers went dead.

Without electricity, people had trouble getting to work, shopping for groceries, and communicating with each other. Normal life pretty much shut down for a few days.

Electricity also plays a crucial role within the human body. A lightning bolt or shock can disrupt or shut down that flow, causing disability or death.

"Electricity is life," says David Rhees, executive director of the Bakken Library and Museum in Minneapolis. The Bakken Museum is dedicated entirely to the history and applications of electricity and magnetism in biology and medicine.

The museum has a lot to keep up with. As scientists learn more about the electrical signals that whiz through our bodies and the electrical pulses that tell our hearts to beat, they are finding new ways to use electricity to save lives.

• **What's in the Bakken Library and Museum in Minneapolis?**

Research on the nervous systems of animals and people are helping scientists design machines that help diagnose and treat brain conditions and other problems. New drugs are being developed to regulate the body's electrical pulses when things go wrong in response to injury or disease.

• **What parts of the body do researchers focus on when they study the human body's electricity? What are some of the goals that these researchers have?**

ELECTRICITY EVERYWHERE

Electricity is everywhere, thanks to the unique structure of the universe. Matter, which is basically everything you see and touch, is made up of tiny units called **atoms**. Atoms themselves are made up of even tinier parts called **protons** and **neutrons**, which form the atom's core, and electrons, which move around outside the core.

Protons have a positive electrical charge, and electrons have a negative electrical charge. Normally, an atom has an equal number of electrons and protons. The

NEWS DETECTIVE   by Emily Sohn

Electricity has saved my life at least twice this year. Both times, I was in the hospital—after a snowboarding accident and after an allergic reaction to a bee sting. Both times, doctors used electricity to take pictures of my brain and bones, monitor my heart, and determine when it was safe for me to go home.

Even when I'm not getting hurt, I'm grateful to have electricity in my life. It powers my air conditioner during the steamy days of summer. It keeps my ice cream cold in the freezer. And, of course, electricity keeps my lights and computer on so that I can write enough stories to pay my bills.

My visit to the Bakken Museum only deepened my appreciation for the wonders of electricity. It was neat to see how people have been marveling at and tinkering with electricity for ages. Even the ancient Chinese practice of **acupuncture** taps into the body's "chi," a source of energy that might be the same as what we call electricity.

Lightning is perhaps nature's most impressive display of electricity. Just be sure you are sitting somewhere safe and dry to watch it light up the sky!

positive and negative charges cancel each other out, so the atom is neutral.

When an atom gains an extra electron, it becomes negatively charged. When an atom loses an electron, it becomes positively charged. When the conditions are right, such charge imbalances can generate a current of electrons. This flow of electrons (or electrically charged particles) is what we call electricity.

• **Describe the difference between a proton and an electron.**

The first person to discover that electricity plays a role in animals was Luigi Galvani, who lived in Italy in the late 18th century. He found that electricity can cause a dissected frog's leg to twitch, showing a connection between electrical currents traveling along an animal's nerve and the action of muscles.

QUICK SIGNALS

• **How did Luigi Galvani know there was a connection between electricity and an animal's nerves?**

All animals that move have electricity in their bodies, says Rodolfo Llinas, a neuroscientist at New York University's School of Medicine. Everything we see, hear, and touch gets translated into electrical signals that travel between the brain and the body via special nerve cells called neurons.

Electricity is the only thing that's fast enough to carry the messages that make us who we are, Llinas says. "Our thoughts, our ability to move, see, dream, all of that is fundamentally driven and organized by electrical pulses," he says. "It's almost like what happens in a computer but far more beautiful and complicated."

By attaching wires to the outside of the body, doctors can monitor the electrical activity inside. One special machine records the heart's electrical activity to produce an **electrocardiogram** (**EKG**)—strings of squiggles that show what the heart is doing (Figure 4.1). Another machine produces a pattern of squiggles (called an **EEG**) that represents the electrical activity of neurons in the brain.

One of the newest technologies, called **MEG**, goes even further. It actually produces maps of magnetic fields caused by electrical activity in the brain, instead of just squiggles.

Recent observations of patterns of nerve-cell action have given scientists a much better view of how electricity works in the body, Llinas says. "The difference between now and 20 years ago is not even astronomical," he says. "It's galactic."

Now, researchers are looking for new ways to use electricity to help people with spinal injuries or disorders of the nervous system, such as Parkinson's disease, Alzheimer's disease, or epilepsy.

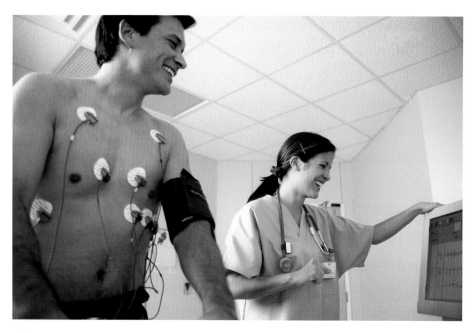

Figure 4.1 An EKG uses electrodes and a computer to record the electrical activity of the beating of the heart.

People with **Parkinson's disease**, for example, often end up having tremors and being unable to move. One type of treatment involves drugs that change the way nerve cells communicate with each other. As part of another new treatment, doctors put tiny wires on the head that send electrical impulses into the patient's brain. "As soon as you put that in," Llinas says, "the person can move again."

Philip Kennedy at Emory University in Atlanta has even invented a kind of "thought control"

- **How do medical specialists treat people with Parkinson's disease?**

to help severely paralyzed people communicate with the outside world. His invention, called a neurotrophic electrode, is a hollow glass cone filled with wires and chemicals. With an implanted electrode, a patient who can't move at all can still control the movement of a cursor across a computer screen.

LOOKING TO THE PAST

One way to help keep the medical field speeding into the future might be to cultivate an appreciation for the past. At least, that's what the folks at the Bakken Museum think.

When I recently visited the museum, Rhees and Kathleen Klehr, the museum's public relations manager, took me down to a huge padlocked room in the basement called "The Vault." Row upon row of shelves were crammed with rare, old books about electricity, early versions of pacemakers and hearing aids, and all sorts of weird devices. One was a shoe-store X-ray machine, powered by electricity, that showed you whether your foot fit comfortably into a new shoe.

Upstairs, the exhibits included a tank of electric fish and Hopi dolls dedicated to the spirit of lightning.

There's also a whole room dedicated to a monster made famous in a book titled *Frankenstein*. Made from

• **Why did shoe stores in the 1950s have X-ray machines?**

assorted human parts, the monster was brought to life by an electrical spark. When Mary Shelley wrote *Frankenstein* in 1818, electricity was still a relatively new idea, and people were fascinated by the possibilities of what they might be able to do with it.

Even today, the *Frankenstein* room, with its scary multimedia presentation, remains one of the Bakken's most popular exhibits, Klehr told me. "It's been centuries," she says, "and everyone is still excited about *Frankenstein*."

That's something you might keep in mind the next time a blackout strikes. Without electricity, those monsters under your bed might have a lot less power over you!

After Reading:

- **Why does David Rhees, near the beginning of the article, claim that "electricity is life"?**

- **Why do scientists refer to the chemical impulses in our bodies as electrical "signals"? What do they signal, and how do they do it?**

- **Why do the employees of the Bakken Library and Museum think the museum will help advance medical research?**

- **Why do you think the *Frankenstein* exhibit is so popular?**

- **Electrical signals inside the human body carry messages to and from the brain. What systems rely on electricity to carry information between people?**

Is Your Cell Phone Harming Your Health?

Everyone knows it's dangerous to talk on the cell phone while driving, but did you know that some scientists believe that cell phones may cause other health problems, such as cancer? As writer Emily Sohn shows in the following article, some studies have found that long-term exposure to the radiation emitted by cell phones causes cancer in laboratory animals. How that might affect you–especially if you use your phone a lot–remains to be seen.

—The Editor

Cell Phones and Possible Health Hazards

by Emily Sohn

Getting a phone call from a friend when you're sick can act just like a steaming bowl of chicken soup. It feels good just to know that someone cares. But if your phone is a cell phone, it's possible that all the chitchat may itself cause some health problems.

Normal phones are harmless because they transmit sound as electrical pulses through those wires that hang from poles or snake through pipes or tunnels underground. Cell phones use a different strategy. Every word you speak into a cell phone becomes a digital message that gets sent out into the air as pulses of **microwave radiation**.

Some people worry that letting all that radiation pulse across your brain can cause serious health problems, including cancer (Figure 4.2). Now, scientists in Sweden report evidence that radiation from some cell phones kills brain cells in rats.

The researchers exposed adolescent rats to low levels of cell-phone radiation for two hours. Fifty days later, up to 2% of cells in the rats' brains were dead or dying, the scientists report.

Figure 4.2 **Some scientists have caused controversy by claiming that using cell phones frequently can cause cancer.**

No one's sure what this means for people. No other studies have so far uncovered significant health effects in animals or people, and other scientists have yet to confirm the Swedish results. Just in case, however, it might be wise to keep your calls short and to use a hands-free headset to increase the distance between you and your cell phone.

Going Deeper:

Morgan, Kendall. "Hold the Phone? Radiation From Cell Phones Hurts Rats' Brains." *Science News* **163 (February 22, 2003): 115. Available online at** *http://www.sciencenews.org/20030222/fob1.asp*.

Medicine Without Injection

Not too many people like getting shots, but we all know how important it is to keep up on vaccinations or to take our medicine when we're sick. Thanks to a new field called "nanoscience" that uses tiny chips and tools to improve all kinds of things, you may never have to get an injection again. In the near future, your doctor might be able to implant a very small microchip into your body, which would release just the right amount of the medicine you need at just the right time.

—The Editor

A Micro-Dose of Your Own Medicine

by Sorcha McDonagh

"I promise, this won't hurt a bit," the doctor says, smiling. Then: jab. You've just gotten another shot.

If getting an injection isn't your idea of a good time, there's some promising news. Scientists have developed an amazing little device that could replace some injections–and pills, too.

The new device is a microchip that can be implanted in your body. The chip is about the size of a dime and is as thin as a piece of paper. On its surface are several small, sealed pockets for storing drug doses. These doses can be released into your body one by one at different times.

Each pocket is sealed with a different type of **polymer**, a material that has very long molecules. (Some of the natural substances in your body, such as proteins, are made of polymers.) By varying the length of the polymer molecules in the seals, the scientists can control when the drugs in each little pocket are released. Seals with longer polymer molecules take longer to break. Seals made with shorter polymer molecules will be the first to break and release drugs into your body.

With an implanted chip, you wouldn't need to

remember to take your medicine because the chip releases the drugs into your body for you, on schedule. The chip would also work well for certain types of vaccines that require several doses. Instead of making lots of trips to the doctor—and getting lots of injections—you'd only need to go once to have the chip implanted, and then the chip would take care of the rest.

So far, Robert Langer and his team at the Massachusetts Institute of Technology have made chips that can deliver drug doses for nearly five months. And after a chip has dispensed all of its medicine, it dissolves slowly inside your body.

This sort of chip isn't available to doctors yet, but when companies start making it, your doctor will then be able to say, "This really won't hurt a bit!"

Going Deeper:

Goho, Alexandra. "Timing Is Everything: Implantable Polymer Chip Delivers Meds on Schedule." *Science News* 164 (October 25, 2003): 260. Available online at *http:// www.sciencenews.org/20031025/fob3.asp*.

You can learn more about polymers online at *www.psrc.usm.edu/macrog/kidsmac/*.

Good Tapeworms?

If you know what a tapeworm is, you know it's not a very pleasant creature. These parasites can get inside the digestive tract of humans and other animals and feed off the things we eat, getting bigger and stronger and continuing to grow for years if not removed effectively. Recently, however, scientists have found out how some kinds of tapeworms manage to stay alive in the hostile, highly acidic environment of the stomach–by producing a special chemical. Thanks to this discovery, researchers are now looking at ways to use this "tapeworm chemical" to create drugs that will help people fight illnesses.

—The Editor

Tapeworms and Drug Delivery

by Emily Sohn

It's not easy living inside an intestine. But some creatures are happiest in the warm and juicy confines of other animals' digestive systems. A tapeworm called *Hymenolepis diminuta*, for instance, can live for years in a rat's intestine, growing up to a foot long (Figure 4.3).

One of the biggest challenges to gut living is all the churning that happens in there. Between meals, the muscles in a mammal's intestine contract rhythmically to flush out waste and bacteria. Somehow, tapeworms manage to slow down the contractions enough to stay inside. They even swim up and down the intestinal tract as food moves through.

Now, scientists at the University of Wisconsin think they've discovered one of the tapeworm's secret weapons: a chemical called cyclic guanosine monophosphate, or cGMP. Research by John Oaks and colleagues suggests that cGMP helps slow intestinal contractions.

The new work may help scientists develop more effective medicines. Because molecules move more slowly through rat intestines that are infected with tapeworms, the scientists think a dash of cGMP could slow down the movement of pills after they've been swal-

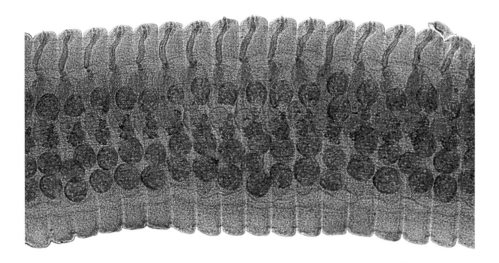

Figure 4.3 This photograph of a *Hymenolepis* tapeworm—one of the many parasitic worms that can attack humans—was taken under a microscope.

lowed. That would give the body more time to absorb medicine in the pills, letting less go to waste.

So, even though the life of a tapeworm might not sound pleasant, studying the icky parasites more might do us some good.

Going Deeper:

Travis, John. "A Tale of the Tapeworm: Parasite Ploy Suggests Drug-delivery Tactic." *Science News* 163 (March 22, 2003): 181–182. Available online at *http://www.sciencenews.org/20030322/fob6.asp*.

Buckyballs

No, buckyball isn't a new sport or piece of athletic equipment, although it does somewhat resemble a soccer ball. A buckyball is an unusual molecule with 20 six-sided patches (like those you've seen on a soccer ball). When it gets inside the human body, it can cause serious harm to cells. As writer Sorcha McDonagh shows in the following article, however, studying buckyballs may help scientists find new ways to protect your health.

—The Editor

Little Bits of Trouble

by Sorcha McDonagh

If you've kicked around a soccer ball, you may have noticed the pattern on the ball's surface. The ball is stitched together from 12 patches with 5 sides (pentagons) and 20 patches with 6 sides (hexagons).

About 20 years ago, chemists discovered that carbon can form into molecules with the same shape. They nicknamed them **buckyballs**. These strong, hollow particles may someday be used to carry medicine or even block the action of certain viruses.

Scientists have now found that buckyballs can harm living cells. Research by Eva Oberdörster, a biologist at Southern Methodist University in Dallas, and her team shows that these molecules damage brain cells in fish.

Buckyballs belong to a group of materials known as nanomaterials. The prefix "nano" means one-billionth. A nanometer is one-billionth of a meter–roughly the width of just five carbon atoms lined up in a row. So, a buckyball is an extremely tiny particle–only a few ten-thousandths of the width of a human hair.

To make a nanomaterial, scientists manipulate individual atoms to build molecules of different shapes. Groups of these molecules form materials with particular characteristics, making them suitable for different jobs. For example, some nanomaterials are already being used in makeup and sunscreens.

Because buckyballs may someday be used in industry, Oberdörster and her team conducted experiments to find out if the molecules are **toxic**.

The researchers added different quantities of buckyballs to water in a fish tank. After 48 hours, they removed the fish from the tank and checked different parts of the fishes' bodies for damage. Although none of them died, the exposed fish showed 17 times as much damage to brain cells as did fish not exposed to buckyballs.

In a separate experiment, Vicki Colvin of Rice University in Houston found that buckyballs damage human cells growing in a lab. But she also found a possible solution to the problem. Coating buckyballs with other kinds of simple molecules appears to make buckyballs safer.

Nanomaterial particles come in all sorts of sizes and shapes, so it's not yet known whether they all have the same harmful effects that buckyballs do. It's going to take a lot more experiments to sort out all the possible health effects of these amazing, new materials.

Going Deeper:

Goho, Alexandra. "Tiny Trouble: Nanoscale Materials Damage Fish Brains." *Science News* 165 (April 3, 2004): 211. Available online at *http://www.sciencenews.org/articles/20040403/fob1.asp*.

Learn more about buckyballs by following the links online at *http://mathforum.org/alejandre/workshops/buckyball.html*.

New Ways to Build Bones

Breaking a bone is a painful experience, and one that takes weeks or even months to recover from. What if scientists could come up with a way to help bones heal more quickly after an injury? In the next article, writer Emily Sohn explores some of the latest ways health researchers are doing just that.

—The Editor

A Framework for Growing Bone

by Emily Sohn

If you've ever broken a bone, you know what a pain the healing process can be. You may end up wearing a cast for weeks, aching and itching as you wait for the fractured bone to get better.

In cases of severe bone damage, surgeons sometimes take bone from one part of the body and use it for repairs in other parts. Thanks to the wonders of bone biology, the procedure works, but it can be painful and expensive.

Now, scientists have invented a promising new material that could help encourage bones to grow back without many of the usual complications.

The researchers, from Switzerland, made a framework structure with a combination of star-shaped molecules, proteins, and protein fragments. Inside the framework, they put proteins called **BMPs**, which spark bone regrowth. When the structure is then attached to the site of an injury, bone-forming cells attach themselves to the framework and dissolve parts of it, allowing BMPs out as needed to fix the bone.

In tests with rats, the new framework structure encouraged bone regrowth in places where fragments of the animals' skulls had been removed.

Someday, the new structure might eliminate the weeks of pain and tedium that most people face after breaking a bone. You'll be climbing trees again in no time!

Going Deeper:

Gorman, Jessica. "Bone Fix: New Material Responds to Growing Tissue." *Science News* 163 (April 26, 2003): 261. Available online at *http://www.sciencenews.org/20030426/fob6.asp*.

ACL: Anterior cruciate ligament; a ligament of the knee that attaches the front of the tibia to the back of the femur.

acupuncture: Ancient Chinese practice of putting small needles in the skin to cure disease or relieve pain.

allergen: Any substance that causes an allergic reaction (an excessive immune reaction that may include sneezing, rash, or inflammation) in sensitive people.

allergies: Excessive reactions of the immune system.

alpha-actinin-3: A protein found in fast-twitch muscle fibers.

anaphylaxis: Hypersensitivity that results from contact with a particular substance; an anaphylactic reaction may be severe, including an inability to breathe and possibly death.

antibiotic: Substance that has the ability to kill or weaken certain types of bacteria.

antibodies: Proteins produced by the immune system in response to an invasion by a disease-causing substance that will allow the body to recognize the same substance in the future and launch a fast response.

atoms: The smallest particle of an element that can exist either alone or in combination.

attention-deficit/hyperactivity disorder (ADHD): A psychological disorder marked by disruptive behavior and problems with learning or paying attention.

bacteria: Single-celled microorganisms that may cause disease.

BMPs: Bone morphogenetic proteins.

buckyballs: Molecules of buckminsterfullerene, a very unstable form of carbon.

coronavirus: A single-stranded RNA virus that has a crown-like appearance.

DNA: Deoxyribonucleic acid; substance that serves as the molecular basis for heredity.

dyslexia: A learning disorder marked by problems in reading, writing, and spelling.

eczema: A skin condition characterized by redness, itching, and oozing lesions.

EEG: Electroencephalograph; a machine that uses electrodes placed on the skull to record brain waves.

EGCG: Epigallocatechin-3-gallate; a component of green tea that has been shown to fight certain forms of cancer.

electrocardiogram (EKG): Tracing produced by an electrocardiograph, a device that records changes in electricity produced by the heartbeat.

enzymes: Special proteins that help cause biochemical reactions in the body.

epidemic: An outbreak of disease.

epidemiology: Branch of medicine that studies the incidence, distribution, and treatment of disease within a population.

Epipen: A registered trademark of Dey; a device that allows a person to inject him- or herself with epinephrine to treat a severe allergic reaction.

fast-twitch muscles: Muscles that contract quickly, particularly during brief high-intensity activities that require strength.

gene: The functional unit of inheritance that controls the spread of traits from one generation to the next.

gray matter: Tissue of the brain and spinal cord that contains both nerve cells and nerve fibers.

histamines: Chemicals that cause the capillaries to dilate, smooth muscles to contract, and stomach juices to be secreted. They are frequently released during an allergic reaction.

immune system: The cells and organs of the body that work together to prevent foreign substances from causing infection and that fight infections that do occur.

intermittent hypoxia: Condition that causes periodic deficiencies in the amount of oxygen in the body, which often results from stopped breathing.

MEG: Magnetoenchephalography; a technique that records the magnetic fields associated with activity in the brain.

microbes: Living things that are too small to be seen without the aid of a microscope.

microbiologist: A scientist who studies microscopic forms of life.

microwave radiation: Energy that consists of short electromagnetic waves, usually between about one millimeter and one meter in length.

mutation: A change in hereditary material that results in either a physical or biochemical alteration.

neurons: Nerve cells.

neutrons: An elementary particle that has no electrical charge.

osteoporosis: A disease that causes bones to degenerate and become prone to fracture.

Parkinson's disease: A chronic neurological disorder characterized by tremor, rigid muscles, problems with balance, and a shuffling gait.

pathogen: A disease-causing organism.

pollen: Dusty microscopic spores in a seed plant.

polymer: A chemical compound made up of repeating structural units.

prefontal lobe: Front part of the brain that is believed to play a role in determining the difference between self-motivation and outside influences.

prions: Protein particles that may cause neurodegenerative diseases.

protons: Elementary particles that have a positive charge.

RNA: Ribonucleic acid; the nucleic acid that is associated with controlling the chemical activities of cells.

temporal lobe: Large portion of the cerebrum located in front of the occipital lobe; it contains the area of the brain associated with the sense of hearing.

tonsils: Two masses of lymphoid tissue on the sides of the throat.

toxic: Poisonous.

vaccines: Preparations of killed or weakened pathogens introduced into the body to help create antibodies and provide protection against the pathogen in the event of later exposure.

viruses: Disease-causing particles that contain genetic material but cannot live or reproduce unless they are inside a host cell.

Further Reading

Books

Darling, David. *Beyond 2000: Micromachines and Nanotechnology: The Amazing New World of the Ultrasmall.* Parsippany, NJ: Dillon Press, 1995.

Ferreiro, Carmen. *Bovine Spongiform Encephalopathy.* Philadelphia: Chelsea House Publishers, 2005.

Friedlander, Mark P, Jr. *Outbreak: Disease Detectives at Work.* Minneapolis: Lerner Publishing, 2000.

Gold, Susan Dudley. *The Musculoskeletal System and the Skin.* Berkeley Heights, NJ: Enslow Publishers, 2003.

Serradell, Joaquima. *SARS.* Philadelphia: Chelsea House Publishers, 2005.

Shorter, Frank. *Running for Health, Fitness and Peak Performance.* New York: Dorling Kindersley, 2005.

Websites

American College of Sports Medicine
http://www.acsm.org/

The Bakken Library and Museum
http://www.thebakken.org/

KidsHealth
http://kidsh ealth.org/

Kids Running
http://www.kidsrunning.com/

National Institute of Environmental Health Sciences
  http://www.niehs.nih.gov/

Neuroscience for Kids
  http://faculty.washington.edu/chudler/neurok.html

Trademarks

Advil is a registered trademark of Wyeth Consumer Healthcare; Aleve is a registered trademark of Bayer Corporation; Benadryl is a registered trademark of the Warner-Lambert Company; EpiPen is a registered trademark of Dey; Frisbee is a registered trademark of Wham-O Incorporated; Tylenol is a registered trademark of McNeil PPC.

Index

ACL 41, 44
acupuncture 105
allergies 2, 26, 27–28, 29, 30–31,
     32–33, 80, 98
alpha-actinin-3 67, 68
American Academy of Pediatrics 79
anaphylaxis 30
antibiotics 48
attention-deficit/hyperactivity disorder
     (ADHD) 17, 18, 19, 20
attention disorders 2

bacteria 7, 47, 48, 50, 70, 81, 82, 96,
     97
Bacteroides thetaiotaomicron 82–83
Bakken Library and Museum 104,
     105, 109, 110
Barrett, Craig 100
Blahnik, Jay 44–45
bone density 75–76
Boston marathon 55, 59, 63, 64
bovine spongiform encephalopathy.
     See mad cow disease.
buckyballs 92, 121, 122, 123, 124
Butte High School 97

cancer 111, 112, 113
cell phones 92, 111, 112, 113, 114
Centers for Disease Control and
     Prevention (CDC) 39–40, 48, 50
Children's Hospital at Montefiore 76
Children's Hospital at Westmead 67
Colvin, Vicki 123
Consortium for Conservation
     Medicine 8
Coupey, Susan 76, 77, 79

Creutzfeldt-Jakob disease (vCJD) 14
cyclic guanosine monophosphate
     (cGMP) 119–120

Daszak, Peter 8, 10
Dew, Mary A. 85
DNA 6, 23, 24, 68
Donnelly, Christl 15
duPont Manual Magnet High School
     99
dyslexia 2, 23, 24–25
DYXC1 24–25

E. coli 81
Emory University 108
epidemics 2, 6, 9, 12
epipens 32

fast-twitch muscles 67
fractures 36, 48, 51, 52, 53, 70, 125,
     126
Frankenstein (Mary Shelley)
     109–110
Full-Body Flexibility (Jay Blahnik)
     44

Galvani, Luigi 106
Grandma's Marathon 59
green tea 99–100

Hegde, Beth 61
Hirpa, Iddoshe 99–100
histamines 30, 32
Hunter, Torii 41
Hymenolepis diminuta 119, 120

page:

3: Science VU/Visuals Unlimited
28: © Corel Corporation (top and lower left); Photos.com Select (lower right)
37: Take 2 Productions/Ken Kaminesky/CORBIS
43: © Lambda Science Artwork
49: © Gary Gaugler/Visuals Unlimited
56: Rene Shenouda/zefa/CORBIS
71: Royalty-free/CORBIS
78: BAUMGARTNER OLIVIA/CORBIS SYGMA
93: Digital Art/CORBIS
108: Royalty-free/CORBIS
113: Simon Marcus/CORBIS
120: © Biodisc/Visuals Unlimited

Contributors

EMILY SOHN is a freelance journalist, based in Minneapolis. She covers mostly science and health for national magazines, including *U.S. News & World Report*, *Health*, *Smithsonian*, and *Science News*. Emily divides her time between writing for kids and writing for adults, and assignments have sent her to countries around the world, including Cuba, Peru, and Sweden. When she's not working, Emily spends most of her time rock climbing, camping, swimming, exploring, and pursuing adventures outdoors.

TARA KOELLHOFFER earned her degree in political science and history from Rutgers University. Today, she is a freelance writer and editor with ten years of experience working on nonfiction books for young adults, covering topics that range from social studies and biography to health and science. She has edited hundreds of books and teaching materials, including a history of Italy published by Greenhaven Press. She lives in Pennsylvania with her husband, Gary, and their dog and cat.